5

"Charles Stone is an excellent writer. I love his work. He hit a hot button with this book for all of us who serve as pastors. The temptation to keep people happy—and be liked—impacts all of our ministries. This is gold, pastors. Pure gold."
Ron Edmondson, senior pastor, Immanuel Baptist Church, Lexington, KY

"Many of us in ministry have been dragging around a ball and chain called people pleasing. It is our constant companion that accuses us and fills us with regret. Charles Stone offers hope and help that can help us break free from our approval addiction."
Lance Witt, founder of Replenish Ministries, author of *Replenish*

"People pleasing is a trap in which many people get caught—especially Christian leaders. . . . Dr. Stone combines solid biblical principles with principles of neuroscience and family/organizational systems to show how people pleasing develops, how it impacts the pastor and those the pastor tries to please, and finally, how to overcome it. I highly recommend this very practical book."
John DeKruyter, executive director, Alongside, Inc.

"Unfortunately, I see many pastors and leaders fall into the people-pleasing trap. . . . Charles provides practical, doable and grace-filled ideas on how to tackle this issue head-on. Supported with Scripture and neuroscience insight, it's a must-read for every pastor in today's high-expectation ministry environments."
Tony Morgan, author, consultant, leadership coach

"Dr. Stone tackles a topic ministry leaders nervously joke about but rarely take seriously. *People-Pleasing Pastors* is an important resource for every ministry leader. Supported by research and made relatable by personal stories, this book will challenge and propel you to lead more authentically and effectively."
Jenni Catron, executive director, Cross Point Church, author of *Clout*

"Charles Stone helps turn John 12:43 pastors ('they loved the approval of man more than the approval of God') into 1 Thessalonians 2:4 pastors ('so we speak not as pleasing man, but God who examines our hearts'). *People-Pleasing Pastors* serves as an important book for those in ministry."
William Jones, president, Columbia International University

"*People-Pleasing Pastors* bridges practice and theory to equip pastors to become not only more emotionally aware of their people pleasing but also competent to navigate their emotions. All ministry leaders . . . will benefit from applying this book to their personal life and the teams in which they serve."
Aubrey M. Malphurs, author, founder of The Malphurs Group

"If you've been a local church leader for more than about five minutes, you know there is a fine line between serving people and pleasing people. And under the pressures of ministry it's often difficult to discern that line. Charles Stone brings profound insight and practical wisdom to help us approach leading and loving others in a healthy and productive way."
Dan Reiland, executive pastor, 12Stone Church, author of *Amplified Leadership*

"Self-awareness in Christian leaders is precisely Paul's point in Romans 12:3. And the lack of self-awareness in leaders is debilitating Christ's church. . . . *People-Pleasing Pastors* is destined to become a central practical training text for all who work in ministry contexts. Truly an equipping book!"

Russell R. Veenker, BCPC, clinical director, Mountain Learning Center

"Charles Stone has that rare gift of knowing and speaking directly to the heart of today's shepherd-leader about the one big leadership issue we all have but rarely admit—our tendency to want to be liked. . . . Churches will be far healthier whose pastors and leaders read this book!"

Brandon Cox, founding pastor, Grace Hills Church, editor, Pastors.com

"My mentor Adrian Rogers used to say, 'If you please God it doesn't matter whom you displease; if you displease God it doesn't matter whom you please.' This insightful book will aid pastors to make sure they are God-pleasers, not people-pleasers."

James Merritt, author, founder and senior pastor of Cross Pointe Church

"Thousands of gifted, called and passionate pastors are lost to the church every year. The reasons vary but high on the list is people pleasing. . . . Stone's insights are remarkable and his applications life changing. This book can save the ministry of a pastor and a church."

Larry Magnuson, SonScape Retreats

"Many, if not all pastors today, often unconsciously, suffer from a vicious 'double bind' of knowing that they are 'to please the Lord' but are hard wired to 'be pleasers of people.' Charles Stone helps pastors and church leaders recognize it, and then begin to cut and unravel the various aspects of this painful and lethal condition of ministry. He can do so because he has struggled with it himself and has found the freedom of becoming a slave to 'one master.'"

Keith Meyer, pastor, author of *Whole Life Transformation*

"Refreshingly honest . . . practical. . . . An excellent tool for self-evaluation. Dr. Stone delivers insightful, empathetic help to all of us who deal with a very common struggle in ministry—the need to please. As one who can relate, I highly recommend this book."

Rusty Hayes, senior pastor, First Free Church, Rockford, IL

"Charles Stone writes about a topic that every person and leader needs to be aware of: people pleasing. He shows the problem and offers seven practical principles as solutions . . . full of wisdom and insights. Reading this book will allow you to become a better leader."

Dan Black, leadership blogger

"I wish Charles Stone's new book, *People-Pleasing Pastors*, had been available to me as a pastor twenty years ago. His proposal that many pastors lead from the perspective of wanting everyone to be happy, stay happy and it's our job to make sure that we please everyone resonated with me. I think it will do the same for many pastors."

Bill Nicoson, president, CEO, Cornerstone Pastor's Network

CHARLES STONE

PEOPLE-PLEASING
PASTORS

AVOIDING THE PITFALLS OF
APPROVAL-MOTIVATED LEADERSHIP

IVP Books
An imprint of InterVarsity Press
Downers Grove, Illinois

InterVarsity Press
P.O. Box 1400, Downers Grove, IL 60515-1426
World Wide Web: www.ivpress.com
Email: email@ivpress.com

Published in association with The Steve Laube Agency, Phoenix, Arizona.

InterVarsity Press® is the book-publishing division of InterVarsity Christian Fellowship/USA®, a movement of students and faculty active on campus at hundreds of universities, colleges and schools of nursing in the United States of America, and a member movement of the International Fellowship of Evangelical Students. For information about local and regional activities, write Public Relations Dept., InterVarsity Christian Fellowship/USA, 6400 Schroeder Rd., P.O. Box 7895, Madison, WI 53707-7895, or visit the IVCF website at www.intervarsity.org.

All Scripture quotations, unless otherwise indicated, are taken from the Holy Bible, New International Version®. NIV®. Copyright ©1973, 1978, 1984 by International Bible Society. Used by permission of Zondervan Publishing House. All rights reserved.

While all stories in this book are true, some names and identifying information in this book have been changed to protect the privacy of the individuals involved.

Cover design: David Fassett
Interior design: Beth Hagenberg
Images: Two men, illustration: CSA Images/Archive/Getty Images
thumbs up icon: © filo/iStockphoto
Vintage Labels: © cajoer/iStockphoto

ISBN 978-0-8308-4109-7 (print)
ISBN 978-0-8308-7190-2 (digital)

Printed in the United States of America ∞

Library of Congress Cataloging-in-Publication Data
Stone, Charles, 1954-
 People-pleasing pastors : avoiding the pitfalls of approval-motivated
leadership / Charles Stone.
    pages cm
Includes bibliographical references.
 ISBN 978-0-8308-4109-7 (pbk. : alk. paper)
1. Pastoral theology. 2. Christian leadership. 3. Motivation
(Psychology)—Religious aspects—Christianity. 4. Social acceptance. I.
Title.
BV4011.3.S75 2014
253—dc23

                    2013040762

P	19	18	17	16	15	14	13	12	11	10	9	8	7	6	5	4	3	2	1
Y	30	29	28	27	26	25	24	23	22	21	20	19	18	17	16	15	14		

I dedicate this book to

my wonderful, supportive wife, Sherryl,

who has made me a better person, partner,

parent, pastor and pastor to pastors.

Contents

Foreword

Since ancient history, idols have existed in all shapes and sizes. All forms of idols fill gaps. We were designed to worship and will worship something. And as strange as items like statues or ancestral markings may appear, it's not hard to notice their power. They capture the identities of those who are so connected to these attachments from their culture and history.

Yet strangely enough, my idols are not strange to me. They call to me personally. They make their persuasive case for why I need them so badly and how much they can do for me. They try to convince me that we can all get along here in one place together, that I can share space with both them and my Christian devotion at the same time, and that God will understand.

My idols are much more personal than a piece of stone or a block of wood. Anything that shapes my identity or fills my thoughts with something other than God, especially on a regular, ongoing, irresistible basis, is an idol. Idolatry does not count the cost of worshiping anything but God. And although few of us could ever imagine worshiping a picture of ourselves, the reality is that we are either worshiping God or some form of ourselves.

Of course, there are the typical idols that come to our mind quickly when we talk about this—things such as greed and lust. But another one that we don't often talk about is the idol of the approval of others. In *People-Pleasing Pastors*, Charles Stone has focused in on approval-motivated leadership, a problem that is all too great in ministry. LifeWay Research data acquired for this work confirms that a high percentage of pastors will admit to struggling with motivation that comes from the desire to please people.

Every idol is a competitor. Our kingdom calling will always be mutually exclusive with the conniving appeals of other gods. We must never forget that we are commissioned by God to live with different loyalties from those of the world—and that, in fact, part of our motivation for choosing this singular existence is for the sake of those who are caught in the enemy's trap.

Because if we allow idols to occupy living quarters in our hearts—especially on a consistent, unquestioned basis—we will never be able to develop the integrity and discernment necessary to challenge the oppressive values of the broader culture. We'll be too distracted and self-absorbed to notice the many examples of pain, doubt, confusion and injustice happening in people's lives right around us.

We are not called to please people so that we can achieve a more secure identity. We are called to love people out of the secure identity that we already possess, the one that was bought for us through the redeeming work of Christ.

People-Pleasing Pastors acknowledges a real problem, and helps equip those in ministry to resist the temptation of seeking the approval of people above all else.

Ed Stetzer
President, LifeWay Research

Acknowledgments

So MANY PEOPLE HAVE INFLUENCED ME in writing this book. First, my family. My wife, Sherryl, and my children, Heather, Josh and Tiffany. Their influence on me has been priceless. My parents, Charles and Doris, have also helped form me into the person I am today.

Thanks to Steve Laube, my agent. He's stuck with me through this, my third book, and offered his wise guidance. I appreciate his professionalism and honesty.

IVP, my publisher, has been a joy to work with. They believe in their authors. Every staff person with whom I've been in contact has shown the utmost willingness to help me and make my book better. Special thanks to Al Hsu, my editor. His knowledge of the business, his promptness in responding to my questions, and his character have been in evidence in every communication.

I thank Dr. Golnaz Tabinia, my professor in my neuroleadership masters program who has taught me much about the brain, one of the foundations upon which I've built the book.

And most importantly, I thank the Lord for gently nudging me to discover not only my people-pleasing tendencies but how to overcome them.

Introduction

I can't give you a surefire formula for success,
but I can give you a formula for failure:
try to please everybody all the time.

HERBERT BAYARD SWOPE,
AMERICAN EDITOR AND JOURNALIST,
FIRST RECIPIENT OF THE PULITZER PRIZE

I GREW UP IN A RELATIVELY NORMAL, middle-class family. We didn't live in luxury, nor were we poor, but we had everything we needed. My parents took me to church every week, and although I "joined" the church as a child, I didn't truly come to faith until age seventeen.

In high school I was skinny, so playing football didn't fit me. As a senior I sat on the bench for seven games and never played. So I quit. As for basketball, I couldn't dribble. And I was afraid of a baseball. But I excelled in school and I enjoyed my social circle: geeks and nerds.

When I started college, I planned to enter politics until God re-directed me into full-time vocational ministry. After I graduated, I began seminary, and within a couple of years the church I had joined hired me as its part-time singles' minister.

It seemed that everything I touched turned to gold in that first ministry; it seemed I could do no wrong. In retrospect, though, my success came because I rode on the coattails of a great pastor and because hundreds of single seminary students attended the church. Unfortunately, this gave me unrealistic ministry expectations. I assumed that success would follow me into the future.

After seminary graduation and a three-year stint in another growing church, my wife and I planted a church in the Atlanta suburbs. I envisioned myself becoming the Rick Warren of the South. Fifty-one people attended our first service, which was in a small ballet studio filled with floor-to-ceiling mirrors. *Fifty-one is pretty good for a first Sunday,* I thought.

I was so successful in the next six months that I worked that number down to seventeen. I was crushed. My vision of a thriving church began to dim.

Despite my feeling disheartened, God blessed the next fourteen years there and we grew a healthy midsize church. Yet I began to develop people-pleasing tendencies. I was driven to grow my church and to avoid failure. I did everything I could to please people, although I didn't realize I was doing it. *After all,* I thought, *if people like me, they'll attend my church.*

I now realize that instead of being driven primarily to please God by a vision he gave me, I easily acquiesced to do what pleased people. Although I never compromised my theology or my morals, I would try to please others and avoid criticism at all costs. I began to lose my identity, and approval-motivated patterns began to take root in my heart, though I was unaware of them.

In addition, our oldest daughter began to rebel. And our youngest daughter was diagnosed with a brain tumor. These family challenges added even more stress to my life and left me with less energy to notice these insidious people-pleasing traits. Although I taught sound theology, applied church-growth principles and practiced spiritual disciplines, a hole was developing in my soul.

I wish I'd known twenty-five years ago what I've written about in this book. I could have avoided a lot of heartache in our family and in the churches I served. I've learned that healthy and successful leadership has little to do with what I can do to get others to like me. Rather, it has everything to do with my identity in Christ, with what's in my heart and my head. What I had assumed indicated success in leadership—limited criticism and people liking me—was the opposite of what actually does. As Edwin Friedman, a highly respected Jewish rabbi who taught extensively on leadership, wrote, "Chronic criticism is, if anything, often a sign that the leader is functioning better!"[1]

People-pleasing, approval-motivated leadership pervades today's churches, as my extensive research for *People-Pleasing Pastors* revealed. When I got the idea for this book, I didn't want to base it simply on anecdotes. Rather, I wanted a strong, objective foundation to support my ideas. That prompted me to commission research on nearly 2,300 pastors, including men and women, young and old, poorly educated and highly educated from large and small churches in North, Central and South America. Seventy-nine percent of pastors in a survey of about 1,000 and 91 percent in a survey of more than 1,200 admitted to people-pleasing tendencies to some degree in their ministries.

This problem extends beyond the church. Because of the fall, everybody struggles with pleasing others. History bears this out. Friedman noted that much of the cause of the Civil War was rooted in presidents who people-pleased.

> It [the Civil War] . . . was ultimately the result of the five
> Presidents before Lincoln. . . . The way in which these glad-
> handling, conflict-avoiding, compromising "commanders-in-
> chief" avoided taking charge of our growing internal crisis
> when they occupied the position "at the top" is exactly the
> same way I have seen today's leaders function before their
> organizations (or families) split.[2]

Christians, perhaps uniquely so, struggle with people pleasing
because we're "supposed to" be sweet and nice. And some profes-
sions, by their very nature, draw people into them because they
offer opportunities to help others. Ministry and politics both fall
into that category. Both pastors and politicians, if rightly motivated,
want to help and serve others. However, that very desire often
makes us most susceptible to people pleasing.

If People-Pleasing Pastors Anonymous existed, I'd probably be a
card-carrying member. I'm still in recovery. In retrospect, as I think
about my thirty-plus years in ministry as a senior pastor, church
planter, teaching pastor and associate pastor—half of that time in
churches with more than a thousand attendees—I can now see the
impact of people pleasing. Not only I have felt its effects, but my
family and the churches where I served have as well.

By most standards, my ministries have been successful. The
churches I served grew numerically, and the people grew spiritually.
We served the community and we served the world. On the whole,
the people felt that I served them well. And I believe we honored
the Lord.

Yet I wonder how the decisions I made that were motivated by a
desire to please somebody in the church resulted in missing God's
best. I wonder how many more people could have moved closer to
Jesus had I not allowed desire for approval to influence my leadership and my decisions. I know I can't wallow in mistakes from
the past. I won't. And I don't mean to imply that I lack a spine or

that I've cowered before every critic. I haven't. Yet I believe that my people-pleasing tendencies may have hindered progress in the churches where I served.

What makes people-pleasing, approval-motivated leadership so detrimental? It's subtle, often counterintuitive and stifling to a spiritual leader's passion and joy if left unchecked.

WHAT IS A PEOPLE-PLEASING PASTOR?

Before I answer that question, consider this fifteen-second exercise. Right now, before reading beyond the next two sentences, quickly think of the top five words or phrases you'd use to describe a people-pleasing leader. Don't spend much time on this. Just let words pop into your mind.

Did you think of any of these or of terms like them?

- weak willed
- indecisive
- plastic smile
- convictionless
- wimpy
- back slapper
- affirmation lover
- crowd pleaser

To some degree, these terms aptly describe a people-pleasing pastor. Yet the ones that might not have come to mind—unyielding, opinionated, defensive, distant, thick skinned, loner or cold—may describe an approval-driven leader as well.

Unhealthy people pleasing is often tricky to see. Most ministry leaders know that we should please God and not people, because the Bible often tells us to avoid it. For example, *The Message* paraphrase sounds an alarm about people pleasing: "There's trouble ahead when you live only for the approval of others, saying what flatters them, doing what indulges them" (Lk 6:26).

Yet it's sometimes hard to know when we actually please God. So, as a tangible way to please him, we try to please people through our service, preaching and leading. When others approve, we assume God approves. But here's where the challenge comes. How do I discern if my motives are rooted in pleasing God or in pleasing others? That's what I hope *People-Pleasing Pastors* will help you do: sort out when your motivation is pleasing God and when you seek to please others in an unhealthy way.

Galatians 1:10 is this book's foundational verse:

Am I now trying to win the approval of men, or of God? Or am I trying to please men? If I were still trying to please men, I would not be a servant of Christ.

It reminds us that the gospel—Jesus is all—should motivate us to please him above all. I've quoted the last third of this verse many times since I began to realize my pleaser tendencies. Although I've known about these tendencies for a long time, I didn't know how to overcome them. Now, in my second half of ministry life, I'm learning how to make the verse more than a trite slogan. I'm learning that with God's grace I can change my approval-motivated tendencies as a leader.

So can you, and that's why I wrote this book. I believe any spiritual leader can change his or her unhealthy approval motivations with the Lord's help. I'm convinced that when leaders pay attention to these tendencies and make changes, they begin to have

- greater creativity
- healthier teams
- clearer vision
- renewed passion
- more internal peace

- clearer decision making
- better conflict management
- decreased anxiety
- less defensiveness
- clarity in hearing God's quiet voice
- more fruit from spiritual disciplines
- fewer mental distractions

Is All People Pleasing Bad?

Not all people pleasing is misguided or unhealthy. Pleasing God and healthy people pleasing are not mutually exclusive. In 1 Corinthians 9, the apostle Paul talks about his freedom as a minister of the gospel. God gives pastors certain rights: being treated with respect and enjoying the spiritual fruits of their labor (both spiritual and material). Yet certain responsibilities counterbalance those rights: preaching willingly, serving others and not being a slave to anyone. Paul captures this tension in this verse.

> Though I am free and belong to no man, I make myself a slave to everyone, to win as many as possible. To the Jews I became like a Jew, to win the Jews. To those under the law I became like one under the law (though I myself am not under the law), so as to win those under the law. To those not having the law I became like one not having the law (though I am not free from God's law but am under Christ's law), so as to win those not having the law. To the weak I became weak, to win the weak. I have become all things to all men so that by all possible means I might save some. I do all this for the sake of the gospel, that I may share in its blessings. (1 Cor 9:19-23)

In other words, Paul committed himself to pleasing others ("to the weak I become weak") if it promoted the gospel. Yet he refused to please people if he perceived doing so would hinder the gospel (see Gal 1:10; 1 Thess 2:4). So, the ultimate test to determine whether or not our people pleasing is wrong is whether or not it promotes the gospel.

Yet we're human, and we want people to like us, so we do things to please them and make them happy. We all want to belong, feel loved and be appreciated for our efforts. God-honoring pleasing also happens when we foster healthy relationships, exhibit the fruit of the Spirit and practice the Golden Rule.

A principle in Scripture reminds us that we get what we give: "Give, and it will be given to you. A good measure, pressed down, shaken together and running over, will be poured into your lap. For with the measure you use, it will be measured to you" (Lk 6:38). So when we treat people with love and respect and "please them" in a Spirit-led way, which pleases God, we often get the same in return. This idea suggests another way to test our people pleasing: we know we've pleased others in a healthy way when they are better off when we do it and when we sense God's peace in our hearts.

Perhaps this topic has spurred you to ask, "What about all the verses that seem to say that I'm supposed to please others?" For example,

> Do nothing out of selfish ambition or vain conceit, but in humility *consider others better than yourselves.* (Phil 2:3)

> In everything I did, I showed you that by this kind of hard work we must help the weak, remembering the words the Lord Jesus himself said: "It is *more blessed to give than to receive.*" (Acts 20:35)

> Honor one another *above yourselves.* (Rom 12:10)

How should we take these truths in light of people pleasing? Does Scripture command us to do the opposite of what I will suggest in this book? If not, how do we serve others, honoring them above ourselves, while also appropriately caring for ourselves?

We get a clue by looking at Jesus' teaching and practice. Although he healed the sick, raised the dead and taught many, he didn't heal every sick person, teach everybody or raise every dead person. He often pulled himself away from the crowds to replenish his soul and be with his Father (see, for example, Mt 14:23; Mk 1:35; Lk 5:16). He took care of himself and didn't try to meet everyone's needs or please everyone who clamored for his attention. He didn't always make himself available. And when he answered a question from a teacher of the law about the greatest commandment, he told us where to focus our love.

> "The most important one," answered Jesus, "is this: 'Hear, O Israel, the Lord our God, the Lord is one. Love the Lord your God with all your heart and with all your soul and with all your mind and with all your strength.' The second is this: 'Love your neighbor *as yourself.*' There is no commandment greater than these." (Mk 12:29-31)

Those of us in ministry usually do a great job teaching how to love God and others. However, it's a bit awkward to teach about loving ourselves, because self-love seems self-serving and self-centered. It's especially difficult for many pastors to love themselves truly. After all, what does it really mean and how do we do it?

Author Harriet Braiker answers this question with a term for loving ourselves: enlightened self-interest. "What this means," she writes, "is that you will take good care of yourself, even putting your needs first at times, while simultaneously considering the needs and welfare of others."[3]

Often we subconsciously tune our internal antenna to the needs of others and constantly scan to find ways to please them, often with a right motive. But we also tend to ignore the antenna that alerts us to our own needs. In a counterintuitive way, by people pleasing we squelch our best and true God-created selves, thus limiting what we should bring to others through our leadership. By minimizing or ignoring loving ourselves, we don't love God and others as we well as we could. So I hope this book will encourage you to examine people pleasing in your life and lead you forward to renewed spiritual vitality.

How the Book Is Organized and Benefits for the Reader

People-Pleasing Pastors is divided into three sections with several chapters in each. In section 1, I challenge you to ask if people pleasing has infected your leadership. Then I unpack what lies at the source of people pleasing and suggest a key to conquering and avoided unhealthy people pleasing, represented through the acronym PRESENT. Section 2 explains the solution: develop into a PRESENT leader instead of a pleaser leader. Practical insights on how to do that fill these chapters. Finally, in section 3, which I've called "The Leader's Toolbox," I offer some tools you can use to help both you and your teams grow in this area.

Two unique features add to the book's value. First, throughout the book are sprinkled real-life stories that I've collected from church leaders who struggle with people pleasing. While I keep the integrity of each story, I changed enough detail to preserve anonymity. Second, I've asked well-known ministry leaders such as Ron Edmondson, Dave Ferguson, Pete Scazzero and Lance Witt for their advice on how to avoid people pleasing. I've included their responses in each chapter as well.

The Three Strands in *People-Pleasing Pastors*

I believe good leadership books should be based on solid footing. I've read many good ones, and I've noticed that the not-so-good ones are based on one-dimensional anecdotes from the writer's life, are too theoretical or simply regurgitate what somebody else wrote.

Although this book does include anecdotes and insights from

other leaders and writers, it's built on three objective strands of truth. I liken it to the metaphor the writer of Ecclesiastes used to illustrate the importance of friendships: "A cord of three strands is not quickly broken" (Eccles 4:12). The three strands on which I've based this book start with the letter B: Bible, brain and Bowen. Let me unpack these 3 Bs.

The most important strand, the first B, is truth about leadership revealed in the Bible. Throughout this book, I've used many Scriptures as well as stories of leaders in the Bible, some who were people pleasers and some who weren't. We'll also look to Scripture to learn how to conquer people pleasing.

The second strand, the brain, represents neuroscience. With the advent of the functional MRI (fMRI), scientists are gaining amazing insights into how the brain influences life and leadership. Through observing the parts of the brain that "light up" under an fMRI when we think, feel and do certain things, we now know that the brain profoundly impacts such leadership functions as teamwork, emotional regulation, decision making, communication and change management. People-pleasing tendencies can impair all these leadership processes. So neuroscience will help inform us on how we can minimize unhealthy pleaser tendencies.

The third strand stands for Bowen, specifically Dr. Murray Bowen, a psychiatrist who in the fifties and sixties developed a new perspective on how people process their internal world, relational issues and difficult emotions, particularly anxiety.[4] In contrast to Freud, who focused primarily on the individual, Bowen applied scientific inquiry as he observed how families processed their anxiety. He called his paradigm *family systems* and developed eight principles of human functioning I'll briefly explain later in the book. Bowen and others have since applied this paradigm to organizational leadership in churches and businesses. We'll see that this not only gives helpful insight into how approval-motivated leadership negatively affects our ministries but also suggests what we can do to improve.

Essentially Bowen said that we all carry around an emotional force field to which others come in contact. Churches, boards and staff teams live in their own unique force fields, and a leader encounters them wherever she leads. How we handle these fields determines the degree to which people pleasing affects our leadership.

So these three strands—the Bible, the brain and Bowen—combine to form a strong, objective basis for this book. Although I've incorporated insight from the last two, I've not written the book as a technical manual on either.

In addition to these three strands, I've included some interesting research. I commissioned LifeWay Research to survey one thousand pastors via telephone. The results provided enlightening insight into how deep people pleasing runs among pastors.

To supplement that research, I used an online tool to survey almost 1,200 pastors by combining the LifeWay questions with the Differentiation of Self Inventory (DSI), developed by a Rhodes scholar. This survey confirmed the first survey's findings, and the DSI portion revealed how pastors lead when they enter the emotional fields of others. Also, hundreds of the pastors anonymously shared stories on how people pleasing had affected their churches, their lives and their families. I've sprinkled these throughout the book, providing true-to-life stories about how these pastors cope with their pleaser tendencies.

Another eighty-seven pastors participated in research to see how well one seldom-used spiritual discipline, mindfulness, could potentially help pastors deal with their pleaser tendencies.

A final thought as you begin: If you Google "tire drag," you'll find an interesting athletic-training concept. When an athlete uses a tire drag, he ties one end of a rope to a tire and the other side to his waist. Then he starts to run, albeit slowly. Some extreme athletes use this training technique, but none of them use a tire drag when they compete. As you would imagine, although you may

Book snapshot. Unhealthy people pleasing is a common leadership problem among today's pastors, affecting more than 70 percent to some degree. Since it acts much like a virus, a strong leadership "immune system" is needed to counter it. By incorporating insight from the Bible, family systems and neuroscience, a pastor can develop a healthy immune system.

Because of the immature ways many of us handle ongoing negative emotions (chronic anxiety), people pleasing is mostly driven by the emotional parts of our brains rather than the thinking parts. When we grow in our emotional maturity (differentiation of self) in both our inner world (thinking and feeling) and our outer world (individuality and connectedness), we are less apt to people please. We mature by developing others and ourselves into PRESENT leaders instead of pleaser leaders.

make progress with a tire drag behind you, your progress would dramatically slow.

When I use people-pleasing, approval-motivated concepts to describe a leader, I'm not implying that he or she won't move their ministry forward if they are a pleaser. However, such leadership will clearly limit forward motion, just as a tire drag slows a runner. So if you want to position yourself for maximum kingdom impact, begin to untie the "people-pleasing drag" from your leadership.

As you dig deeper into the book, keep in mind how the following Scripture contrasts a people-pleasing life with a Jesus-pleasing one:

> For my part, I am going to boast about nothing but the Cross of our Master, Jesus Christ. Because of that Cross, I have been crucified in relation to the world, set free from the stifling atmosphere of pleasing others and fitting into the little patterns that they dictate. (Gal 6:14 *The Message*)

SECTION I

The Problem
of People Pleasing in
the Church Today

1

Has the People-Pleaser Virus Infected Your Leadership?

We speak as men approved by God
to be entrusted with the gospel.
We are not trying to please men but God,
who tests our hearts.

THE APOSTLE PAUL (1 THESS 2:4)

I<small>T ALL BEGAN WITH</small> a pig farmer's son.

As an insecure high school student, Dale dreaded living the rest of his life in his dad's footsteps as a poor pig farmer. As a brief diversion from his worries, he attended a Chautauqua movement event. This movement in the late nineteenth and early twentieth centuries brought great speakers to various parts of the country to speak on important topics such as faith or culture. As Dale listened that day, a flame ignited in his heart: perhaps public speaking could be his ticket out of poverty.

When Dale entered college, he began to hone his speaking skills. Other students took note and began to ask him to train them to

become better speakers. When he finished college, America's bur-
geoning economy offered opportunities for salespeople who, with
good people and communication skills, could earn a good living.
After a brief stint selling beef, Dale set up his own school and business
to help other businesspeople overcome their insecurities and become
better speakers. He named it after himself, the Dale Carnegie Institute.

Susan Cain explores his life in a chapter in her seminal book
Quiet: The Power of Introverts in a World That Can't Stop Talking. She
believes that his rise to stardom helped shift our culture's focus
from character to personality, which "opened up a Pandora's Box of
personal anxieties from which we would never recover."

> In the Culture of Character, the ideal self was serious, disci-
> plined, and honorable. What counted was not so much the
> impression one made in public as how one behaved in private.
> The word *personality* didn't exist in English until the eigh-
> teenth century, and the idea of "having a good personality"
> was not widespread until the twentieth.
>
> But when they embraced the Culture of Personality, Amer-
> icans started to focus on how others perceived them. They
> became captivated by people who were bold and entertaining.
> "The social role demanded of all in the new Culture of Person-
> ality was that of a performer," [Warren] Susman famously
> wrote. "Every American was to become a performing self."[1]

Self-help books became popular at this time, not only for the
benefit of salespeople, but also to help people deal with their insecurities so they could become more likeable. Although character
was still important, external charm and personality took center stage.
According to Cain, historian Warren Susman compared the words
used in advice books and magazines from the early twentieth century
to the character guides used in the nineteenth century and noticed a
striking difference. Words such as *duty*, *honor*, *morals* and *integrity*
were replaced with words such as *magnetic*, *stunning*, *attractive* and

> **Chapter snapshot.** In this chapter I use the metaphor of a virus to help us understand that just as a virus hurts the human body, so people-pleasing leadership hurts the body of Christ and reduces the impact of the local church. I included some of the research findings to make the depth of the problem clear. You will be able to identify your level of people pleasing through a simple self-evaluation.

energetic. As Cain notes, "It was no coincidence that in the 1920s and the 1930s, Americans became obsessed with movie stars."[2]

One of the most striking print ads during this time embodied this personality focus. One Williams Shaving Cream/Aqua Velva aftershave ad depicted a debonair, smartly dressed man with an ivory-toothed smile who effused confidence. It was emblazoned with the headline "CRITICAL eyes are sizing you up right now."

This cult of personality swept not only the business world but the church world as well, even before Dale Carnegie made his mark. Richard Hofstadter, one of the United States' most renowned historians, often said that "the star system was not born in Hollywood but on the sawdust trail of the revivalists."[3] The apostle Paul, who apparently wasn't a great speaker himself, would have taken issue with a "star system" rooted in becoming likeable so as to please people. He wrote, "Figure out what will please *Christ*, and then do it" (Eph 5:10 *The Message*).

I don't mean to imply that Carnegie didn't provided great services for thousands of people through his life and company. Yet this message from the son of a pig farmer may have been the genesis for the people-pleasing, approval-motivated leadership prevalent in the church today. Just as a virus causes swine flu, so leaders can be infected with a people-pleasing virus.

But before getting into that, let's take a look at a biblical people pleaser.

Take a few moments to take this brief quiz to discover to what extent this pattern may have taken hold in your leadership. Check the ones with which you agree. Be honest with yourself.

- ☒ In my church's board or leadership meetings, sometimes I don't speak up on an issue for fear of creating tension.

- ☒ I say yes too easily to others' requests for me to do things. Later I regret having put so much on my plate.

- ☐ In meetings I often wait until others explain their views. I do this not because I want to show respect to them, but because I want to hear what they have to say first in case I need to adjust my views to avoid conflict.

- ☐ I go out of my way to attempt to change someone's mind who wants to leave my church or ministry.

- ☒ Too often I repeatedly try to convince someone to agree with my view on an issue, even when it appears he really doesn't want to listen to my opinion.

- ☐ Sometimes I get angry with myself for not having stood up or spoken up for what I believe.

- ☐ I have kept a nonperforming staff person or volunteer leader too long before making a change.

- ☐ When I need to be firm with someone, I delay the conversation. After I do have the conversation, I realize I didn't say everything I should have said.

- ☒ Sometimes I try too hard to be nice.

- ☒ With some people I carefully measure my words.

- ☒ Deep inside I believe I can get most everyone to like me.

- ☒ It bothers me when I upset someone. I tend to blame myself for his distress.

- ☒ I try very hard to keep things peaceful and calm at home and in leadership meetings.

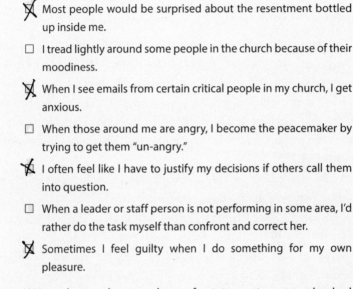

☒ Most people would be surprised about the resentment bottled up inside me.

☐ I tread lightly around some people in the church because of their moodiness.

☒ When I see emails from certain critical people in my church, I get anxious.

☐ When those around me are angry, I become the peacemaker by trying to get them "un-angry."

☒ I often feel like I have to justify my decisions if others call them into question.

☐ When a leader or staff person is not performing in some area, I'd rather do the task myself than confront and correct her.

☒ Sometimes I feel guilty when I do something for my own pleasure.

Write down the number of statements you checked here: _12_

How many did you check? If you checked more than three or four, you've made a good choice by reading this book. I encourage you to apply the principles that follow so you can improve the way you lead.

The Bible's Most Prominent People-Pleasing Leader

The essence of the gospel centers on a commitment to please God above all else. The apostle John records Jesus' words as he preached the gospel and spoke about who we should seek praise from.

> I do not accept praise from men, but I know you. I know that you do not have the love of God in your hearts. I have come in my Father's name, and you do not accept me; but if someone else comes in his own name, you will accept him. How can you believe if you accept praise from one another,

yet make no effort to obtain the praise that comes from the only God? (Jn 5:41-44)

Unfortunately, one of the most prominent characters in the Bible, King Saul, the first king of ancient Israel, failed miserably to please God first and foremost. Although he showed tremendous leadership promise, a serious character flaw led to his failure. Rather than seeking healthy *respect* from others, *validation* from others fueled his leadership. Saul embodies the essence of a people-pleasing leader.

We begin to see his steady downfall when he refused to heed the prophet Samuel's instructions to wait for him before offering sacrifices to God (1 Sam 13). Israel's archenemies, the Philistines, were preparing for battle when Saul's men assessed the situation as hopeless and began to defect. In his fear, he offered sacrifices without Samuel being present, hoping God would come to their rescue. Saul was disobedient again in a subsequent battle, cutting corners by not fully obeying God's instructions to destroy another of Israel's enemies, the Amalekites.

After Samuel confronted him, Saul's response revealed his character crack: "I've sinned. I've trampled roughshod over God's Word and your instructions. I cared more about *pleasing the people*. I let them tell me what to do" (1 Sam 15:24 *The Message*). Saul's people-pleasing tendency led to continued compromise and ultimately to his suicide.

I'm not implying that all people pleasing leads to such extremes, but it will lead to diminished leadership and dampened passion, which the writer of Proverbs captures: "The fear of human opinion disables" (Prov 29:25 *The Message*).

What the Research Shows

Appendix C details the three-phase research that included input from over 2,300 pastors. To summarize again, LifeWay Research performed the first phase: a telephone survey of 1,002 pastors. Phase 2 was through an online survey of more than 1,200 pastors. And the third survey was through a seven-day research project with eighty-seven pastors. The research revealed how deeply people-pleasing, approval-motivated leadership has infected ministry leaders.

It's worth mentioning that research has inherent limitations. While the studies corroborated each other's findings, self-reporting reflected how a respondent felt at the moment the survey was taken. And online research (the last two studies) generally can yield more honest responses; when asked to share weaknesses, most of us would rather do it anonymously.

In summary, the research discovered that 79 percent of the 1,002 pastors in one survey and 91 percent of pastors in the other admitted to people pleasing in their church at some level. Sixty-six percent of pastors in the initial survey and 78 percent in the second survey admitted that people pleasing hindered ministry effectiveness. The survey allowed pastors to pick one of six broad problem areas that they believed their pleaser tendencies affected. The responses they gave are below. (The totals add up to more than 100 percent because pastors could check more than one problem.)

- Difficulty in leading the church as you believe you should: LifeWay, 25 percent; online, 38 percent

- Difficulty in accomplishing personal and spiritual goals: LifeWay, 27 percent; online, 34 percent

- Difficulty with the lay leaders in your church: LifeWay, 27 percent; online, 30 percent

- Difficulty in handling the same situation down the road: LifeWay, 25 percent; online, 28 percent (In the LifeWay sample of pastors in churches with attendance of more than 250, 37 percent said this was an issue.)

- Difficulty with your staff: LifeWay, 21 percent; online, 24 percent

(In the LifeWay sample of pastors in churches over 250, 38 percent said this was an issue.)

- Difficulty in your family: LifeWay, 14 percent; online, 19 percent

A caveat: Conquering and avoiding people pleasing does not mean we become self-absorbed, selfish, self-centered or insensitive to others. God's call to service means that we often should put others first. In that sense we should please them. But serving must never degenerate into servility. Also, the Bible instructs every follower of Jesus to be filled with his Spirit and to live out the fruit of the Spirit: "love, joy, peace, patience, kindness, goodness, faithfulness, gentleness and self-control" (Gal 5:22-23). Living that way will please many. So leaders must appropriately please others and avoid the unhealthy kinds of pleasing.

One of the biggest shocks from my research was the large number of anonymous stories pastors shared about their experience with people pleasing: I collected *one hundred pages* of stories. I've summarized a few below and interspersed others throughout the book. These stories came from pastors across North and South America from small and large churches. As you read them, ask yourself if you've seen similar struggles in your leadership.

Loss of confidence

I recall addressing a group of powerbrokers in a past church, and then when it looked like the issue would not go away and they were becoming more and more militant, I started to back off. I didn't press issues I would have ordinarily pressed as a matter of principle. It shook my confidence and made me angry. I started thinking more of survival than advance, and both the church and my own ministry suffered for it.

Vision confusion

Early in ministry we planted a new congregation in northern Nevada. When calling on potential members, we would ask them what they were looking for in a church. I would often find myself telling different families that we would be the sort of church they were describing, even when that was completely at odds with a promise I may have made the night before on a different visit. I was so committed to pleasing everyone that in my mind the promises were incompatible. The result was a ton of agenda disharmony and vision confusion in the core group and a lot of emotional turmoil for me.

Church division

I gave in to some leaders who wanted to put a particular layman on the board, whom I had previously blocked. He caused nothing but trouble for the next few years, nearly leading us into a church split. I vowed to never put someone who showed any hint of divisiveness in a key position again.

Quitting the ministry

In a church that I pastored, there was a major power struggle with several members who remained very close friends with the previous pastor, who actively worked to wield control through these members. I often felt unable to measure up, always trying to "minister" to these folks in hopes that I could win them over and yet being angry that I couldn't. After two years I left the church and left the ministry. I felt like a failure as a pastor and as a husband/father.

Loss of momentum

I once tried to appease my core leaders when I sensed a need to start a second Sunday service. I delayed the decision for months, trying to work through people's personal issues and make my case. In the end, the ones I tried to appease (or find consensus with) left the church. We started the second service, but a lot of momentum had been lost. This story sort of finalized something I've been learning all along. As a leader, when I seek consensus or appeasement in a situation, rather than lead from a place of principle and vision, I abdicate my authority and nobody "wins."

Delay the inevitable
I had allowed an individual to continue giving leadership to a ministry despite the past fallout of this person's leadership style. My appeasement resulted in having to be involved "once again" with those who were hurt by this person's callous control of others.

HAS THE PEOPLE-PLEASER VIRUS INFECTED YOUR LEADERSHIP?

Edwin Friedman, a contemporary of Murray Bowen, was also a strong proponent of applying family systems insight to religious leaders. In his insightful book *Failure of Nerve,* he draws parallels between the negative emotional processes in organizations, including churches, with what viruses and cancer cells do to the human body. These parallels help explain that people pleasing can damage our leadership.

First, good cells in our bodies do certain things to keep us healthy.

- They specialize for the greater good of the body.
- They self-regulate. They don't go off half-cocked doing what they want to do.
- They communicate with each other.
- Rather than compete, they cooperate.
- They know when their time is up, because they have a gene for self-destruction that activates when needed.

But viruses, unlike healthy cells, work against the body's health. Since they can't self-regulate, they destroy healthy cells by infiltrating them like a parasite and sucking the life from them.

Another pathogen, the cancer cell, actually provides an even better metaphor to describe how people pleasing can hurt our leadership. My youngest daughter, Tiffany, was diagnosed with a brain tumor at age one. Twenty-six years later, after six brain surgeries and an experimental device implanted deep in her brain, she is now doing well. We'll never know what caused the tumor, but we understand some of the characteristics that make cancer cells deadly. In several ways, Tiffany's tumor cells subverted the good processes of normal cells.

- Her unhealthy cells had no ability to self-regulate. They went on a growth spree with no respect for the healthy part of her brain. They invaded the life and space of the good cells. Had I not noticed a twitch in her eye that led to a CAT scan and a tumor diagnosis, the cells would have continued to replicate themselves, ultimately taking her life.

- They did not colonize or group into a brain structure that was growing for her body's common good.

- They were rogue cells, unconnected to and uncommunicative with the good cells.

- They were living for themselves, and if left alone they would have ravaged her brain.

- They reproduced indiscriminately, with no higher purpose in mind.

- They did not know when to quit. It took surgery and radiation to remove and kill them.

Essentially, both viruses and cancer cells do their deadly work because "their behavior and their direction are determined by what is outside rather than what is within."[4] In like manner, people-pleasing leadership gets its direction and behavior from outside (people we strive to please) rather than from inside (personal values, convictions and vision). It can be as deadly to our souls and our leadership as a cancer cell can be to our bodies. However, it's important not to view difficult people as viruses. Instead we must see the unhealthy patterns to which they (and we) can sometimes succumb as the problem.

Do you see the parallel? We set up unhealthy emotional processes in our ministries when we try to placate others through choices like these:

- Allow those with no respect for our boundaries to suck the life out of us, letting them invade space with their self-focused demands.

- Try to make them happy even though they don't have what it takes to be happy, just as a virus or cancer cell has no ability to self-regulate.

- Inadvertently allow them to take us down, just as viruses commit biological suicide by taking out good cells when they die.

Peter Steinki explains how Dr. Paul Brand extended the apostle Paul's analogy of the body in 1 Corinthians when he substituted the image of cells for the image of the body. Dr. Brand said that cells can live either for the benefit of the whole or live for themselves. Often those we try most to please are selfish; they don't really want what is best for the whole, but what is best for themselves. In Brand's words,

> The body is one unit, though it is made up of many cells. If the white blood cell should say because I am not a brain cell, I do not belong to the body, it would not for this reason cease to be part of the body. If the muscle cell should say to the optic nerve cell, because I am not an optic nerve cell, I do not belong to the body, it would not for that reason cease to be a part of the body. If the whole body were an optic nerve cell, where would be the ability to walk? If the whole body were an auditory nerve, where would be the sense of sight? God has arranged the cells in the body, every one of them, just as He wanted them. There are many cells, but one body.[5]

One pastor described how his people-pleaser virus took him hostage and what he finally did to rectify it:

> A man with a strong personality and opinions felt he spoke for a large segment of the church. When decisions were made that he did not agree with, he immediately voiced his opinion, usually with an implied threat of a revolt if the decision did not change. It affected my ministry, because I knew that while he would follow through, I did not know how many would follow him. It reached a point that before making decisions I would ask myself how he would respond and would often avoid going against it.
>
> This issue culminated with one key decision I made about which he disapproved. I made it very clear that I was going ahead with the decision. As predicted, he tried to create a revolt and even contacted our denominational headquarters, who came to assess the situation. In their assessment they found that while a small group supported him, as a whole they strongly supported my decision. They encouraged him to leave the church or get on board and stop what he was doing. He chose to stay, but my actions kept him quiet from that point on. It was a turning point for the church, and a long phase of growth soon followed.

People pleasing can take a tremendous toll on your vitality, joy and effectiveness. But counteracting the people-pleaser virus is not easy. There are no quick fixes. Getting rid of boundaryless staff or getting leaders with new blood won't solve our internal heart issues and patterns. It's a scientific fact that viruses are impervious to new blood. And passively ignoring the problem won't make it go away.

However, we aren't doomed to repeat the past. The solution lies in the power of the gospel as the Lord helps us develop a healthy immune system (see chapter 3). I take great comfort in the life of Timothy. The apostle Paul encouraged him not to be timid (2 Tim

1:7), as apparently he struggled with people pleasing. Yet as his life and ministry unfolds through the pages of Scripture, we see that he became a bold servant of Christ as he experienced his transforming power.

Before we look at the specifics that help us avoid approval-motivated leadership, we must understand how it takes hold in our lives and our leadership, the topic of the next chapter.

RON EDMONDSON'S TAKE

Ron Edmondson, one of today's most prolific leadership bloggers (ronedmondson.com), is lead pastor at Immanuel Baptist Church in Lexington, Kentucky (ibc-lex.org). He offers these wise words to help us avoid and conquer people pleasing:

> You have to be confident in your calling. Ultimately our calling as pastors is not to a church, or even a church's vision statement, but to a person: the person of Christ. When I consistently remind myself of who I am in Christ, I can focus my attention on pleasing Him instead of pleasing every member of my church. It's a daily discipline, but this perspective allows me to better navigate through all the demands placed on me, discerning which ones help accomplish the mission of the church and which ones are merely a distraction.

YOUR TAKE

- To what degree would you say the people-pleaser virus has impacted the leadership of friends you know who serve in the ministry?
- How has the people-pleaser virus affected your leadership?

2

What Makes Leaders Sick?

If they be . . . men pleasers
or men fearers . . . they cannot take
hold of the Church nor the world for God.

E. M. BOUNDS

THE MELTED HANDS of a wristwatch, frozen at 5:56, told the sad story. The tragedy that struck at Mann Gulch would be forever seared into the history books.

The summer of 1949 left Montana as dry as a tinderbox. In a rugged central region of the state lies Mann Gulch, so named by Lewis and Clark. At around noon on August 5 of that year, a fire began. James O. Harrison, a local fireguard, was the first to notice it. He fought it on his own for four hours before Wagner Dodge, a firefighting foreman, and about a dozen firefighters arrived, having been dispatched via a C-47 plane.

In turbulent conditions with a temperature that hit ninety-seven, Dodge gathered his men and told them to eat and prepare their equipment while he scouted the fire. After surveying the situation and meeting with Harrison, he met the men as they made their way down the gully. Because the intense heat kept the firefighters from getting any closer than one hundred feet, Dodge changed his plan. He instructed the men to move from the front of the fire by crossing over to a thinly forested area so that they could then attack it from behind, with the safety of the Missouri River at their backs.

Soon afterward, balls of fire began to leap the gulch. Then the wind swept off the river, and as it combined with the intense heat, it created what firefighters call a blowup, a wall of fire that develops when a fire rapidly grows. With their escape route to the river blocked by the growing conflagration, Dodge ordered his men to begin a retreat back up the gulch.

Realizing, however, that the fifty pounds of equipment that each man shouldered would keep them from outrunning the fire, he ordered them to drop their gear and stop. For whatever reason, whether the inferno's roar muffled his voice or because he broke protocol by telling them to shed their gear, the men continued to try to outrun the fire.

In a moment of clear thinking, Dodge turned, faced the fire, quickly lit a match and dropped it to the ground, burning a small area around himself. He lay face down in the burned-out circle cleared by his fire and covered his face with a cloth. As the fire rounded the corners of that small area, it roared past him. Dodge survived unscathed.

Chapter snapshot. In this chapter you'll see that poorly managed anxiety (a term I use to describe negative emotions in general) lies at the root of people pleasing. I will explain how anxiety rises from the fight-or-flight mechanism and how it essentially shuts down the part of the brain we must access to think clearly, avoid people pleasing and lead well. You'll see that the Bowen paradigm can help us understand how both nature and nurture influence our pleaser tendencies.

But a few seconds later, the racing fire consumed thirteen of the men. Only Dodge and two others survived.[1]

Dodge's technique has now become standard training protocol for firefighting. He faced the fire; the other men did not. The two contrasting reactions led to opposite results, giving us a memorable picture of how pastors often deal with ministry fires.

WHAT FUELS PEOPLE PLEASING

We pastors face fires in our churches every day. Some fires are small and can be contained easily, like a broken copy machine (unless it's Friday and the bulletin hasn't been printed). Others carry much greater consequences, like a staff person discovered in an affair or an elder board asking a pastor to "leave the meeting while we discuss a personnel matter about you."

Anxiety always accompanies ministry fires to some degree. We can do as Dodge did: face our anxieties and thoughtfully respond. Or we can run from them or ignore them and face the painful consequences of doing so. People pleasing has become one of the most common ways pastors "run" as a way to cope with anxiety and unpleasant emotions.

Seminary taught me about sound theology, effective evangelism, sermon preparation, discipleship methods and much more. But I didn't learn how to deal with my own emotionality or that of others in the church. I didn't learn how my brain contributes to my anxiety or how I fit into emotional processes. What do I do when the board treats me unfairly? How do I handle nasty rumors? How should I respond when I get an angry email or a scathing unsigned letter?

I erroneously assumed that if I obeyed God's will with a pure heart, people would like me and my ideas, and they would readily follow my leadership. What a surprise awaited me when I entered ministry. I discovered this fiery ball of emotionality I'm calling *anxiety* not only in my own soul but also in the souls of church board members, church staff and church people in general. Seminary did not prepare me for this. As a result, I often used people pleasing to make it go away, or so I thought.

Harriet Braiker, author of *The Disease to Please*, penned an insightful definition of people pleasing: "a set of self-defeating thoughts and flawed beliefs about yourself and other people that fuels compulsive behavior, that, in turn, is driven by the need to avoid forbidden negative feelings."[2] *Anxiety* is a term that embodies those negative feelings.

So, what do I really mean when I use the word *anxiety*? I use it as an umbrella term for all the unpleasant emotions we can feel, such as anger, fear, worry, anxiousness or depression, often in response to situations where we feel threatened. It's a fundamental human sensation that we don't like, and we unconsciously try to make it go away, often in unbiblical and unhealthy ways.

For people-pleasing pastors, such anxiety can rise before a board meeting, before we speak, after we've had a difficult conversation with someone, when we hear another church's success story or after we've experienced a disappointing Sunday service. Anxiety may rise from actual events or from events we make up in our minds. How we deal with our own anxiety and how we respond to the anxiety in our church affect how well we lead. So let's unpack the term.

Peter Steinki colorfully describes it this way:

> Anxiety comes from an interesting family of words. The great-grandfather is the Greek word *ananke*, meaning "throat" or "to press together." In fact, *Ananke* was the name of the Greek god of constraint who presided over slavery. *Ananke* was the word used for the yokes or rings on the necks of slaves. Anxiety can hold us back, take us by the throat, and chain us like a slave.[3]

An unhealthy response to anxiety, whether it's ours or someone else's, will suffocate, constrict and limit our energy, passion, drive and leadership. In this chapter we'll look at the two kinds of anxiety, what they look like in us and how they show up in an anxious church.

Again, I've built this book on the 3 Bs: the Bible, brain and Bowen. Each thread gives us insight into anxiety. The Bible often cautions us to avoid it and when we experience it to respond in a Christ-honoring way. Bowen considered anxiety to be one of the core components in family systems. And brain research tells us that a deeply imbedded part of our brain, the amygdala, is the primary source of our anxiety. When we leave anxiety unchecked, the thinking part of our brain (the neocortex) loses its effectiveness. When that happens, leadership and relationships suffer.

My research revealed fascinating insights into how we pastors respond to anxiety. The second phase involved an online survey tool that 1,200 ministry leaders took, including pastors, board members and missionaries. It asked questions about how pastors self-assess in areas of maturity that relate to people pleasing. It included a forty-six-question inventory called the Differentiation of Self Inventory (DSI) designed to reveal to what extent some concepts in Bowen's family systems theory show up in our lives.

Murray Bowen coined the term *differentiation of self*, which essentially describes emotional maturity. The DSI probes four specific measures of maturity, all related to how we handle anxiety. I rename them here for simplicity's sake.

- *Emotional control* (called emotional reactivity in the DSI) measures how well a leader thoughtfully responds to stress, problems and anxiety rather than reacting to them.

- *Convictional stance* (called I-position) measures how well a leader stands up for his convictions when pressured to do otherwise.

- *Connectedness in difficulty* (called emotional cutoff) measures how well a leader stays relationally connected to difficult people in anxious times rather than emotionally or physically distancing from them.

- *Healthy independence* (called fusion) measures a leader's ability both to avoid over-involvement with or over-reliance on others to confirm her personal beliefs, decisions and convictions, and to hold clearly defined convictions.

I've likened the properties of a virus or cancer cell to the way people pleasing works. From a biological perspective, neither of these two types of cells can damage a good cell without the good cell's cooperation, at least to some degree. Likewise, when we don't handle our anxiety properly, we subtly cooperate by giving people pleasing an entrance into our lives. However, when we appropriately handle our own anxiety (people please less), we can actually help calm our group's or our church's anxiety. (In the next chapter we'll look at how a healthy immune system protects us from people pleasing.)

Often we respond to anxiety at a subconscious level. Authors James Rapson and Craig English write,

> Nice people become preoccupied with the emotional states of those around them, usually without being conscious that they are doing so. This preoccupation can be exhausting. They don't choose to obsess about what others are thinking and feeling: they simply can't shut it off. As with all anxiety conditions, the thoughts, feelings, and fantasies are compulsive, unbidden, and mostly out of awareness.[4]

Anxiety's power begins with lack of awareness. Kevin Cashman writes about our hidden belief systems in his book *Leadership from the Inside Out.* He suggests seven "shadow clues" that may indicate that shadow beliefs are influencing our leadership.[5] These shadow clues often fuel our anxiety. I've paraphrased them into seven questions related to ministry leadership. Take a moment to ask yourself these questions. If you answer yes to any of them, anxiety could be a stronger influence in your leadership than you realize.

- Does my perspective on what's happening in the church often significantly differ from how key leaders see things?

- Do I often feel stuck, not knowing what to do next?

- Have my ministry strengths *often* become counterproductive?

- Am I resistant to new information or insight from staff, lay leaders or others?

- Do I react in a disproportionate way to difficult church situations?

- Do I react in a judgmental or critical way to others' limitations?

- Do I feel pain or discomfort in some part of my body for no apparent reason?

UNDERSTANDING ANXIETY

Anxiety packs a powerful punch in the church and in our lives. In high school science we learned a concept called *homeostasis*, which means to "stay the same." *Equilibrium* is another word that captures this idea. God created our bodies to regulate levels such as temperature, pH and blood sugar so that under normal conditions they stay about the same. When those markers get out of line, the body attempts to bring them back into balance, into the homeostatic state. Just as our body activates certain processes to seek balance, the emotional systems in our churches, boards, employees and so on seek to strike a balance when anxiety rises. Groups don't like anxiety any more than individuals do.

As a leader, by default pastors *are* in the emotional systems of their board, their staff, their volunteer teams and their church. When we try to bring change or a crisis occurs, that system is often thrown out of balance. Issues such as fear of a new ministry philosophy, a core church member who is upset or a perceived loss by people if certain changes occur can throw the church or the team off balance. Anxiety rises, and forces of homeostasis kick in.

In others words, people feel the status quo has been challenged.

When that happens, and we as leaders begin to feel anxiety rise within us, we're tempted to placate others to make the anxiety go away. However, it's important to know that not all anxiety is bad. It depends on the kind.

Anxiety falls into two categories: acute and chronic. Acute anxiety is an automatic reaction to a real or perceived threat. One Sunday, between our two morning services, a couple who had recently joined our church caught me to share something they had just experienced in our parking lot. They had pulled up next to a rusty, white van when a tall, "creepy-looking" man stepped out and began to talk to them. They said he acted like he was on drugs. With beady eyes he told them he lived in his van by the river. Well, maybe he didn't say *river*. They then pointed in the direction of our worship center and said, "There he is, right there."

Immediately I felt my face flush, my heart rate jump and my anxiety level rise. I thought, *Is this guy going to go off on us today?* I immediately asked our usher team and a couple of plainclothes policemen who attended our church to keep their eyes on him. To say the least, my head was not in my sermon that Sunday. Fortunately he didn't do anything weird—that day. A few months later when I was gone one Sunday, he stood up during the service and challenged the speaker. I guess it was a good day to be absent.

I experienced anxiety that day because God created my brain to respond that way. When we feel threatened, the fight-or-flight part of our brain (the amygdala) instantly heightens our physiological responses in case we need to protect ourselves or others. We need that kind of anxiety. Fortunately, soon after my encounter that Sunday, my anxiety dissipated. This kind of anxiety, prompted by a discrete event, is normal and not harmful unless we react (more about reacting in chapter 10). The issue that causes acute anxiety is usually time based or situational and passes quickly.

The apostle Paul felt acute anxiety, and it was reflected in his letter to the church at Philippi. He deeply loved this church, and they loved him. Philippians reflects his deep concern about their concern for his condition. He emphasizes this when he writes about Epaphroditus, "Therefore I am all the more eager to send him, so that when you see him again you may be glad and I may have less anxiety" (Phil 2:28). He sent Epaphroditus to them so that when the news of his condition calmed their hearts, his anxiety about them would calm as well. In this case, his anxiety appropriately reflected valid concern.

However, the other category of anxiety—chronic anxiety—lies at the root of approval-motivated leadership. With chronic anxiety, the anxiety gets stuck on automatic pilot and seems impossible to shake. Akin to white noise, it creates a constant buzz in our souls. Several years ago, my wife and I took some friends to a Christmas concert by the Trans-Siberian Orchestra. It was an amazing concert, except for one thing: the deafening volume that projected from the bus-size speaker array. We sat right in front of those speakers. And I got a mild case of tinnitus, an incessant white noise in my ear that won't go away.

Chronic anxiety feels much like mental white noise. It constantly weighs on our souls, just beyond our conscious awareness. Yet it causes us to feel slightly off-kilter. As a result, the smallest issues can sometimes push us over the edge. Over time, chronic anxiety creates thinking patterns about which we're often unaware, like grooves of anxiety imbedded in our souls.

Neuroscientists have coined a term for habit formation: Hebb's law, named after the scientist who discovered that brain cells that "fire together wire together." Chronic anxiety takes on a life of its own independent of what originally triggered it, often creating a subconscious habit. Our emotional response to a church event or a difficult relationship issue often does more to raise our anxiety than the event itself.

Here's an example how Hebb's law works with anxiety and people pleasing. A fictitious young pastor we'll call James is serving at his first church, where the lay leadership structure is a deacon board. James learned great theology from seminary, but very little about what to expect from boards or how to handle conflict. His first meeting shakes him.

Several board members come across very harsh and opinionated at this meeting. James tries to make a point, but each time he does his ideas get shot down. Yet when he verbally agrees with the deacons, even though internally he doesn't agree, they respond with smiles and affirmation. Subconsciously he begins to acquiesce regularly to these deacons to keep the peace, thus forming some subconscious thinking and relating patterns.

Now when James attends meetings, he constantly scans the deacons' eyes and body language to gauge the meeting's emotional temperature. Based on what he senses, he knows when to speak up and when to remain quiet. He finds that being a nice guy makes the meetings go better. And he feels better, at least in the meetings. So even though he may disagree with a decision or want to go in a different direction, he doesn't speak up. He puts on a smile and nods. Yet the next day he berates himself for not saying anything. Resentment slowly builds in his heart.

James begins to notice something else. The day the deacons hold their monthly meeting, he always has to take a heavy dose of ibuprofen to stop a headache. His wife and kids also notice that he becomes irritable with his family on those meeting days. This cycle repeats itself for the entire five years he is pastor of this church: headache, irritability, meeting, smile, acquiesce, resentment the next day.

His anxiety in this setting is stuck at a high level; it is the chronic kind. He rarely speaks his mind. He wants to keep the peace so the deacons will like him. But inside he feels frustrated and angry that he doesn't speak up. His body shows it, and his family feels it. Hebb's law has taken effect. His subconscious thoughts and patterns have begun to wire more permanently into his thinking. But those thought patterns can be changed in the same way they were formed.

James finally gets an opportunity to move to a different church, which he does. When he takes this church, he hopes things will be different. In some respects they are. He finds the deacons at his new church much more amenable. However, he still gets head-aches and is irritable toward his family on the day the deacons meet. He feels anxious going into the meeting and unconsciously smiles, nods and scans the deacons' faces, trying to gauge their emotional temperature.

His anxiety does not come from a real threat like what he experienced from his previous deacon board. Rather, it comes from an imagined one, caused by the people-pleaser grooves in his thinking. Neither the deacons nor the meeting itself causes or heightens his anxiety. The pattern of chronic anxiety he developed that he tried to quell by pleasing his former deacons is still with him. And it is affecting his peace and hurting his body.

We now know that chronic anxiety causes what scientists call allostatic load, or wear and tear on the body. Such prolonged stress causes sustained high levels of the stress hormone cortisol. Too much cortisol, along with an overabundance of other hormones and neurotransmitters, can lead to these problems: impaired im-munity, weight gain, greater emotional reactivity, heart problems, decreased memory and diminished brain functioning.

Obviously we should seek to minimize chronic anxiety in our lives. Yet when we allow anxious patterns built around people pleasing to become a subconscious part of our thinking, they hinder our leadership effectiveness and leak into our families. Our family of origin also influences how we deal with anxiety. However, by God's grace we can change these patterns by building a healthy leadership immune system.

When anxiety runs high in our church, board or staff, we face three choices, according to Steinki: instant solutions, short-term fixes or adaptive change.[6] People pleasing runs strongest with in-

stant solutions. Our reactionary brain takes over. Because we want
to calm the board, the staff or the church instantly, we panic and do
what brings immediate relief, even though those choices reflect
little reflective thinking and don't solve the problem. With the
short-term fixes, we don't panic, but people pleasing still runs
strong, so we choose a solution that soothes feelings and makes
people feel good, yet never gets to the root of the problem. Finally,
leaders who lead according to principle practice adaptive change,
which is deep, long-lasting, healthy change. They courageously
and thoughtfully act out of their principles, not to placate feelings
but to do what is best for the church.

Several years ago in an elders' meeting in our church, one of the
elders made a statement that implied I lacked a certain competency
in my role. I don't remember the specific issue, but I clearly remember my reaction. When he made that statement, I impulsively
blurted, "I do not do [whatever it was]!"

He retorted, "You do it all the time."

I immediately jumped out of my chair, stomped over to the sink
area behind me and in anger said, "I never can please you. Everything I do is just not good enough for you, is it?" For the next five
minutes, angry, anxious emotions flew back and forth until the fi-
nesse of another elder helped us cool down.

What happened? I had felt chronically anxious toward this elder
for some time, even feeling anxious when I would see an email
from him in my computer's inbox. And at the time our elder
meetings hadn't gone well. When I felt attacked, my reactionary
brain took over. My emotional reactivity came out as impulsive
defensiveness; it happened without me even thinking about it.
And that's what happens with chronic anxiety. Pressures push us to
react rather than to respond thoughtfully and biblically.

In retrospect, I should have paused and allowed the thinking
side of my brain to control my response instead of the emotional
side. Instead my emotions acted faster than my thinking. I didn't

handle my feelings responsibly so I lost objectivity and civility. My unhealthy drivenness to please this leader and the ensuing chronic anxiety caused an unnecessary conflict.

In reality, his comment probably carried a grain of truth in it. Had I been more thoughtful, more self-aware and less anxiety-filled that I had disappointed him, the conversation could have turned in a constructive direction. Fortunately, we both cooled down, and I apologized for my reaction. As Steinke writes, "Someone *has* anxiety if acute, someone *is* anxiety if chronic."[7] Chronic anxiety causes a low threshold of pain, and in this case, a high chance that I would react when pressured or pushed, which I did.

Edwin Friedman extended the effects of chronic anxiety to groups and organizations. He said that these five fundamental issues characterize chronic anxiety in an anxious group:

- *Reactivity*: when people constantly react to each other, thus creating a vicious cycle
- *Herding*: when forces of togetherness overshadow individuality, causing the church/team to adapt to the least mature member(s) (think of a herd of cows that mimics the reactions of one spooked cow)
- *Blame displacement*: embracing a victim mentality rather than taking ownership
- A *quick-fix mentality*: a drive that causes leaders to focus on symptom relief rather than adaptive (positive) change to relieve leadership/organization pain
- *Lacking well-differentiated (mature) leaders*[8]

Below I've applied those five observations to churches and included qualities that might give clues that your church or team is chronically anxious. As you read them, check the ones that seem to apply to your situation.

Reactivity

- Disunity and conflict in your staff, leadership or church that is overt or lies just beneath the surface
- Lack of mutual respect for each other's boundaries
- Issues getting overblown; small things becoming big
- People taking offense easily
- Lack of love, respect and reasonableness
- Threats (for example, "Do this or I will leave the church")

Herding

- Differing opinions squelched
- People adapting to the least mature (the spooked cow)
- Inordinate attempts to oil the squeaky wheel
- Seeking peace at the expense of progress
- Being satisfied with no less than 100 percent agreement with 100 percent of the decisions

Blame displacement

- Wishing a staff person or church member would leave so things could be better
- Victim mentality
- Focus on problems rather than on solutions
- "You" statements during conflict
- Blaming the "straw that broke the camel's back" rather than looking at the condition of the camel's back
- People/leaders having a difficult time seeing the part they play in the problem

Quick-fix mentality

- Low pain threshold that prompts leaders to seek a quick fix to a problem
- Simplistic answers and solutions to problems
- Tendency to embrace the latest church-growth fad
- A church with a history of terminating pastors, thinking that a new one will fix things
- Secret meetings

Lacking well-differentiated (mature) leaders

(This characteristic is both a product of and a contributor to the first four.)

- Leading from crisis to crisis
- Leadership that clings to an idealized notion of ministry
- Leaders feeling they have to prove themselves constantly
- Leaders mentally rehashing what they said to others and then wishing they had said something different
- Leaders doing nice things for others and secretly hoping those people will reciprocate
- Leaders constantly turning their thinking, feeling and acting dial to the needs of others, hoping to manage the impression those people hold of them
- Leaders driven to be "nice" to everybody
- Leadership that demands certainty
- Bossy leaders who attempt to force others to see their way
- Leadership fails to take unpopular stands
- Leaders who strive for kudos, applause and affirmation
- Leadership unable to step back and view things outside of another person's emotionality, thus reducing vision clarity and stifling creativity

- Leadership that takes responsibility for the moods of others
- Delayed decision making

THE DEADLIEST FORM OF PEOPLE PLEASING: NARCISSISM

Most leaders struggle with balancing healthy people pleasing with unhealthy pleasing. It's the condition we all face this side of heaven. Because of the fall, a pleaser exists in all of us. Yet one version of people pleasing can become toxic and is classified as pathology: narcissism.

Ancient Greek mythology gives us the source of the word *narcissism* and its meaning. As the myth goes, Narcissus was a hunter. As a boy, his face seemed chiseled from the purest marble. His beauty attracted others to him, but they never could seem to get close to him, even though they tried to reach him with their love. He had found another love.

At age sixteen, as he walked along the mythical river Styx, he stopped to take a sip of water from a calm pool. As he knelt, the image he saw in the pool transfixed him. His new love was the image of himself. The story says that because he could not bear to leave his reflection, he lay down by the pool and pined away for himself. His obsession with his own image kept him from giving or receiving love from others. Eventually the earth absorbed him, and he became a narcissus, a flower. Thus the word *narcissism* connotes a fixation with oneself.

Essentially narcissism describes a person with an inflated sense of self-importance and an insatiable drive to be liked and to be the center of attention. Narcissistic leaders create a false self to cover their fear of humiliation. Exposure to the real person would be anathema to them. Their drive to avoid disclosure often results in these kinds of behavior:

- Rage if he experiences shame, for shame exposes his true self
- An inordinate need for praise in order to feel important

- The feeling of entitlement to special treatment
- The immense need for continual feedback of how important he is
- The feeling of superiority and its reinforcement from others
- Strong reaction to rejection and disapproval, sometimes intense rage
- The lack of the capacity to mourn, a defense against depression
- Calculating and conniving behavior to "maintain" supplies of continuous adulation
- An impaired capacity for commitment
- No capacity for self-focus or self-examination[9]

Unfortunately, ministry can tempt us toward narcissism because we are often in the limelight. In the past two decades, it seems that every year a well-known pastor commits adultery or fails in some public moral way, often rooted in narcissistic tendencies. Steinki worked with sixty-five pastors who had affairs and found that narcissism lay at the root of most of those failures. He wrote, "Their acute need for the mirroring of self-importance and for praise was sexualized."[10]

Unfortunately narcissists often exude qualities we laud: self-confidence, a magnetic personality, strong platform skills and the ability to motivate others. While these qualities certainly don't make someone a narcissist, they often accompany such a personality.

If you sense that narcissism may be creeping into your heart, please get help today from a wise counselor. Otherwise, you could become a statistic.

In this chapter we've seen that ministry fires can fuel chronic anxiety, which lies at the root of people pleasing. In the next chapter I explain how a strong inner core—a healthy leadership immune system—can protect us from anxiety-driven people pleasing. We'll look at how to strengthen our inner core through clarifying our values and convictions.

DAVE FERGUSON'S TAKE

Dave Ferguson, lead pastor of Community Christian Church (communitychristian.org) and movement leader of the NewThing Network (newthing.org) offers these wise words to help us avoid and conquer people pleasing:

> Hire your brother to pastor the church with you. . . . He will not let you get away with anything and will call you on whatever people-pleasing or unhealthy practice he sees. That sounds funny but it has been true for me!
>
> And if you can't hire your brother, be sure to build a strong leadership team starting with your inner circle of 3-5 people that you like and with whom you enjoy doing life together. You need to give permission to this team to call you on anything including people-pleasing or unhealthy practices and vice versa. Together, this team can help create a more healthy community and better accomplish the Jesus Mission.

YOUR TAKE

- How would you rate the degree of anxiety you experience due to ministry?

- How do you deal with it?

3

*A STRONG LEADERSHIP
IMMUNE SYSTEM*

> *What lies behind us and what lies ahead
> of us are tiny matters compared
> to what lies within us.*
>
> HENRY S. HASTINGS

CALLED "THE SAVIOR OF WOMEN," his discovery laid the groundwork for one of the most important medical discoveries ever.

Ignaz Semmelweis, born to a wealthy family in Hungary in the 1800s, planned to become a lawyer but, while in school, abruptly switched his career to medicine.[1] After completing his degree, he began work as a surgical assistant at the Vienna General Hospital, which provided two free clinics where poor women, including prostitutes, could deliver their babies.

He noticed a striking difference in the maternal mortality rates between the two clinics. In the clinic staffed by interns who also performed autopsies, the annual mortality rate averaged more than 10 percent. At the other, staffed primarily with midwives, it was close to 2 percent. Pregnant women knew about each clinic's reputation, and many would get on their knees and literally beg for permission to have their babies delivered in the one staffed by the midwives.

Semmelweis was puzzled and deeply troubled by the high mortality rate. Doctors usually attributed it to a disease called puerperal fever, but he was not convinced. As he pondered these deaths, he surmised that somehow the doctors and interns who performed the autopsies and then delivered babies had contaminated the women in the delivery process. He assumed the contamination came from particles on their hands from the autopsy. At the time, germ theory was unknown.

Semmelweis's hunch prompted him to require the interns to wash their hands in a chlorinated lime solution before delivering babies. The mortality rate at that clinic, extremely high that year, plunged from 18 percent to 2 percent within two months after they began washing their hands. As a result, Semmelweis began to publish articles in medical journals about the importance of this simple practice.

Unfortunately the medical profession rebuffed him, perhaps because many doctors felt it beneath their status as "gentlemen" to consider that their hands were unclean. Semmelweis's vocal expression of his convictions ultimately led to his dismissal from the hospital.

Incensed at their refusal to embrace this practice, he began to write vehemently and speak out against the medical establishment, even accusing doctors of being murderers. Over the ensuing years, Semmelweis's deepening depression caused erratic behavior. His wife and others committed him to an asylum, and in an ironic twist of fate, two weeks after his admission he died from a disease akin to the very one he had sought to eradicate. Fortunately, years later Louis Pasteur confirmed germ theory and thus vindicated Semmelweis, placing him in the history books as a pioneer of antiseptic procedures.

Semmelweis had discovered that something unseen was compromising the immune system of these pregnant women that in turn caused needless deaths. In a parallel way, people pleasing often infects our leadership in unseen ways. To counter the problems that the people-pleaser virus can cause, we must learn new habits and embrace biblical values that protect and strengthen our leadership immune system. If we don't, we may become guilty of the same fatal attitude that prompted those doctors to ignore Semmelweis's admonishment. Their pride blinded them from reality.

In fact, the term "Semmelweis reflex" was coined years after his death. It describes a person's reflexive rejection of new information because it contradicts his established beliefs or views. I hope pastors who read this book will consider that an approval motivation might be hindering their leadership rather than react with a Semmelweis reflex.

Chapter snapshot. In this chapter we look at the leader's immune system and the key to protecting it from the people-pleasing infection. You'll see that to counter the people-pleaser virus, we must build a healthy leadership immune system. Bowen would call this immune system *differentiation of self,* what we would usually call *maturity.* I explain that two domains influence a healthy leadership immune system:

- *Interpersonal:* independent versus dependent, the ability to be separate from yet connected to other people in your relationship circle
- *Intrapersonal:* thinking versus feeling, the ability to experience our emotions appropriately yet not let them cloud clear thinking

I conclude this chapter by summarizing the steps we can use to strengthen our immune system through what the acronym PRESENT represents.

In review, three objective strands of truth I call the 3 Bs form the basis for *People-Pleasing Pastors*. The most important and core strand, the Bible, provides the lens through which we view the other two Bs: the brain and Bowen. Here I'll more thoroughly unpack Bowen's concepts, which I've only summarized so far, to provide a framework for future chapters. Although Bowen died in 1990 at seventy-seven, his work resulted in a fresh approach, in contrast to Freudian psychological theory, to understanding our emotions and how we function in our pastoral leadership.

Dr. Murray Bowen began his formal psychiatric training in 1946 at the Menninger Clinic in Topeka, Kansas. After completing his work there, he conducted research at the National Institute of Mental Health in Rockville, Maryland, from 1954–1959 on families that had a schizophrenic family member. He then taught and did research at Georgetown University School of Medicine's Department of Psychiatry in Washington, D.C., until his death. His paradigm leads us to a different way of thinking.

THINKING "SYSTEMS" VERSUS THINKING LINEARLY

Bowen used scientific inquiry to look for similarities in how different species functioned and also studied how biological, psychological and sociological processes interconnected within families. By unraveling the relationship patterns in families he studied, he replaced cause-and-effect, linear thinking (like how billiard balls bounce off each other on a pool table) with systems thinking.

He when he began to treat people with psychological problems, he did it differently than those with a Freudian perspective. Freud explained human emotionality in individual terms. He believed each person was autonomous and that inner psychological conflicts and mechanisms rooted in childhood experiences motivated him or her.

Although as Christians we certainly are individuals, the Bible most often describes us in the context of community. In the Old Testament, we understand community in the context of the Israelite nation. In the New Testament, we understand it through Paul's description of the body of Christ. Although Bowen didn't ignore a person's individuality, he placed the individual into a larger context, a system.

In my view, his perspective more closely aligns with the biblical view that we are individuals vitally connected to others in community. Our primary community is our physical family and our community of faith. However, pastors are also in a community with boards, staff and other influencers in the church. It's important that we see ourselves and our emotional functioning (and others' functioning) in that larger context. The lens of systems thinking can help us see that interconnectedness.

I learned about systems through my undergraduate degree in systems engineering. However, Bowen extended that thinking into the family, and others have applied it to church leadership. Understanding systems helps a leader see how all the parts and relationships in a ministry relate and how his leadership affects it.

For example, linear thinking would assume that if Elder A reacted to you in a leadership meeting, it was simply because you said something that prompted his reaction. Systems thinking, however, takes a broader look to see more at work in the relationship, not simply attributing the reaction to something you said. This perspective would view each of you as both influencer and influenced—not as cause and effect, like the billiard ball effect I mentioned above, but more like feedback loops. You certainly might have said something that in the moment prompted Elder A's reaction. However, unseen dynamics may also have been at play to cause his reaction.

Understanding systems can help a pastor understand how interactions with people become patterns, both good and bad. It takes the big-picture perspective to view both how one person or group mutually influences another and the patterns that rise out of those interactions.

Bowen's paradigm views the family (or staff team or elder board) as the emotional unit, rather than as an individual, as would Freud. When the emotional functioning of one member of a family or board changes, it causes a compensatory change in another part of that family or board member, much like how a decorative mobile works. If you touch the top part of a mobile, the effect reverberates down the mobile into its other parts. Likewise, if you touch a part at the bottom of a mobile, the movement reverberates upward, although it's not as pronounced.

This illustrates the pivotal place leaders play in the system we're in, be it among elders, staff or volunteers. Since a leader usually fits somewhere near the top organizationally, what he does often causes change down the line. If he is spiritually and emotionally healthy (has a strong leadership immune system), what he does reverberates down the line to the benefit of his team. As the saying goes, "A rising tide lifts all boats." Likewise, if his immune system is not healthy, what reverberates down the line will negatively affect others.

Eight core principles summarize Bowen's paradigm.[2] Below, used with permission, are Dr. Emyln Ott's questions that describe Bowen's principles. I've also placed in parentheses the term he used for each. Before his death, he worked on a ninth principle: spirituality. Unfortunately he never completed it.

- How well are family members functioning with their whole selves (differentiation of self)?

- Who and what gets worried about (family projection)?

- When relationships get wobbly, what happens and are those relationships stuck (triangles)?

- How do relationships between siblings and parents create expectations and dynamics (sibling position)?

- What patterns and emotions seem to be carried on to multiple generations (multigenerational transmission process)?

- What happens when there is no contact with ideas or people (cutoffs)?

- What is the impact of societal pressures (emotional process in society)?

- How do anxiety and togetherness function (emotional system)?

In the next several chapters we'll look at some of these principles through a biblical lens. And we'll apply them to functioning as a leader in the context of people pleasing.

Emotional Maturity: The Key to a Healthy Immune System

The first Bowen concept I listed above, differentiation of self, is the fundamental building block for the strong leadership immune system we need to combat people pleasing. We can't ignore people in our churches who incessantly try to change us, just as we can't avoid germs or viruses in our environment. But we can strengthen our body's immune system so that when it's exposed to a pathogen, our body can fight it off.

Likewise, we can strengthen our leadership immune system so that when we're tempted to people please, we don't become complicit with others by strengthening their influence through yielding to their demands or giving in to their emotionality. Medically, pathogens lose their power when a host cell refuses to give in. Likewise, when we refuse to give in to people pleasing, those pushing us to change lose their power over us and over our ministries.

Dr. Roberta Gilbert, one of the country's most well-known experts on family systems theory and its application to pastoral leadership, calls self-differentiation the *cornerstone* concept.[3] I define differentiation of self as "emotional maturity" and will use the phrases interchangeably. To capture the broad spectrum and nuances of differentiation of self, Bowen developed a 0 to 100 scale to describe it. A score of 0 would indicate someone with no differentiation (somebody in a morgue), and someone with a score of 100 would be perfect. Jesus is the only person who would be a 100.

By combining Bowen's scale with scales others have used, I've created a brief self-assessment below so you can evaluate where you see yourself on the emotional-maturity spectrum. As you take the assessment, write down the number beside each statement that would represent how you assess yourself in that category. The far left of the scale represents "Always true of me," and the far right represents "Never true of me." In other words, if you would answer question 1 as "*It is always true of me* that I tend to be emotionally driven and find it difficult to distinguish fact from feeling," you would write down the number 1. If it were never true of you, you'd write down 4. If it were sometimes true of you, you'd write down either 2 or 3, depending on how frequently that statement is or isn't true of you.

Always true of me			Never true of me
1	2	3	4

3 — I tend to be emotionally driven and find it difficult to distinguish fact from feeling.

3 — I have to feel loved to function best.

2 — I easily react and get defensive, especially when under stress.

3 — I tend to shirk responsibility for my behavior.

2 — I find it hard to bounce back quickly from anxiety-producing events.

3 — It's tough for me to stay the course when pressured by others to do otherwise.

3 — When someone disagrees with me, I find it difficult to stand on my principles.

3 — In emotional times, it's difficult for me to calmly state and stand on my convictions.

2 — When others disagree with me, I tend to relationally disconnect from them.

3 — When under pressure, it's hard for me to make decisions.

2 — My feelings soar with approval and drop with criticism.

3	I tend to spend a lot of energy trying to get people to like me and validate me.
3	My thinking gets foggy under stress.
2	I often insist that others conform to my wishes.
3	My thinking tends to be black/white and either/or.
3	I look for quick fixes to problems to decrease anxiety.
3	I'm usually not very teachable.
2	I'm not very self-aware of my thoughts and feelings and of how I come across to others.
2	I can be rigid.
2	It's difficult for me to stay emotionally neutral.
3	I tend to take things personally.
3	It's difficult for me to keep perspective, especially under stress.
2	I have difficulty keeping boundaries with others.
3	I'm pretty clueless about how others perceive me.
2	It's difficult to listen to others who are anxious, angry or defensive without reacting to them.
65	**Total score**

If you're like me, your score probably fell somewhere in the middle (minimum score=25, maximum score=100). Most pastors aren't deeply emotionally immature, yet we all have room to grow. Although the inventory has no specific score that indicates a serious problem, the higher our score, the more emotionally mature we are and the stronger leadership immune system we possess. Growing into maturity to become more like Jesus (sanctification) takes a lifetime. If we remain teachable and aware of our strengths and weaknesses and rely on his Spirit, he will transform us so that we become more spiritually, relationally and emotionally mature. As Bowen would put it, we will grow our differentiation of self.

THE TWO MATURITY SCALES

Essentially two domains comprise differentiation of self (emotional maturity) and thus influence our immune system: the *inter-personal domain* and the *intrapersonal domain*. Figure 3.1 illustrates these two.

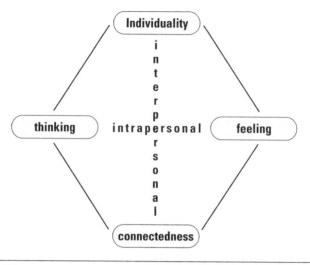

Figure 3.1.

The intrapersonal part (our inner world) includes thinking and feeling, our thoughts and emotions. The interpersonal (our outer world) involves individuality and connectedness, being both separate and together with others.

First, healthy differentiation of self means that you can closely connect to others (that is, your staff, board, church members), yet remain an individual with your own views and identity that is not glommed into the group's thinking. The apostle Paul writes about this in 1 Corinthians 12. He says that although we are part of the body of Christ, we also have unique and separate roles and gifts. A pastor who understands and accepts how God uniquely fashioned him won't be as motivated to seek others' approval. He understands that he is a separate person yet connected to and in community with others. His rootedness in Christ enables him to live in the world without threat of losing himself.

Second, with a healthy differentiation of self you can emotionally connect with others and appropriately express your own emotions in the face of another's emotionality, but not allow your feelings to control you. Even though you may fully feel your negative emotions, you don't let them cloud your thinking. A strong leadership immune system relies on the Holy Spirit to control thinking so that the pastor responds to life's challenges with grace rather than reacting to them. It's a direction in life, not a destination, because we never "arrive" this side of heaven. An emotionally and spiritually healthy leader (high differentiation of self) builds a healthy capacity for thinking/feeling in his intrapersonal world to manage the tension he experiences in his interpersonal world of togetherness/separateness.

Pastors with a lower differentiation of self experience more chronic anxiety and more problems in life, and they tend to react or acquiesce to others when facing stress and conflict. Their feelings cloud their thinking, and they often lead from subjectivity rather than objectivity. Those leaders also lose their individuality by giving away parts of themselves to others through catering to people's whims. When they lose their individuality, they exchange a part of themselves with others, hoping to manage and decrease their own anxiety.

Because such a leader wants to make his negative feelings go away, he loses a part of himself in the process when he people pleases. The lower a pastor's emotional maturity, the more he will live in and be led by his emotional world. He will wrap his goals around comfort, security, happiness and feelings of love. Because he hungers for those pleasurable experiences, he invests his energies to gain others' approval through people pleasing.

A pastor's story below describes how low differentiation of self can limit leadership effectiveness.

I had a former music minister's wife confront me about something I said in a sermon. Rather than affirming that what I said was what I believed, I hemmed and hawed about it. Eventually, we let her husband go and then discovered that there was a great deal of "undercurrent" behind our backs. We lost a number of people.

The sermon criticism wasn't so much a theological one. Rather, seeds of discontent prompted her criticism. I feel like if I had been firmer in supporting what I had said in the sermon, it would have created an opportunity for the discontent to come out into the open then. Our church would have been healthier in the long run had I done so.

A pastor with high emotional maturity (a strong leadership immune system) can experience healthier relationships with leaders, staff and church people. Why? Because he chooses to allow wise, biblical thinking to guide how he relates rather than letting his emotions dictate. He has rooted his self-worth in his relationship with Christ and in his values, not in tension-free relationships, good circumstances, approval from others or a growing church. He keeps his focus even when things aren't going well. He is able to say "I" in the face of others who try to coerce him to say "we." He can stay the course when reactive people want to reroute him.

The more separate and individual he is as a leader, while at the same time staying connected to others, the more clearly he can define reality and lead others in it. He is more often fully present with others, yet still maintains his individuality.

AVOCADOS AND MATURITY

One way to visualize differentiation of self is to picture an avocado. If you cut it in half, you see the mushy green stuff and the pit. It doesn't take much effort to remove the mushy part of the avocado. You can easily spoon it out or scrape it off. However, you can't do the same with the pit. You can't easily cut it or change its shape. Why? Because it's solid.

A pastor with a strong spiritual and emotional core (strong leadership immune system) is like that large, solid seed in the avocado. He certainly must have a soft side, but at his center he is solid, in the good sense of the word, rather than unyielding. However, a pastor with low differentiation of self, a people pleaser, has a much smaller inner core and a much larger squishy part. He easily morphs and adapts to the pressures around him and loses parts of himself when he tries to please others. And of course he could go in the other direction and become too solid—that is, unyielding and inflexible.

Bowen contrasted these two parts, calling one a solid self and the other a pseudo-self:

> The solid self says: "This is who I am, what I believe, what I stand for, and what I will or will not do in any given situation." The solid self is made up of clearly defined beliefs, opinions, convictions, and life principles. . . . The pseudo-self is composed of a vast assortment of principles, beliefs, philosophies, and knowledge acquired because it is required or considered right by the group.[4]

The more emotionally and spiritually mature a pastor is, the more differentiated she will be. She will give in to people pleasing less often. I've contrasted solid-self qualities with squishy ones in the list below. As you read them, circle one statement in each line that would best describe you. After you do, commit to the Lord that you will work with him to develop your solid self.

- Principle based or circumstances driven
- Stands on principles or changes to avoid displeasure
- Does what is right or keeps the peace to keep others happy
- Conviction or comfort
- Authentic or pretending

- Clings to God when pressured or acquiesces to others when pressured
- Listens to disagreement or gives in to it or becomes defensive
- Stays connected to critics or either fuses with them or cuts off the relationships
- Carefully considers differing viewpoints or quickly embraces them to avoid someone's displeasure
- Thoughtfully responds or automatically reacts
- Leads through conflict or strives to make it go away quickly
- Stays put in a church or changes churches a lot
- Stands on his own two feet or is wobbly and uncertain
- Solid yet flexible or porous and inflexible

In the remainder of the book we'll look at practical ways to grow our differentiation of self (emotional maturity) that in turn will strengthen our leadership immune system. I'll also unpack the acronym PRESENT. PRESENT leaders seek through their leadership to stay fully present for others instead of being distracted by mental chatter that thinks, *How can I please you?* They carry and present themselves with confidence, poise and character. PRESENT leaders freely offer their leadership as gifts to the church instead of using it to get from others what they want. They present themselves as leaders to others in a God-honoring way. Finally, PRESENT leaders embrace these qualities and practices:

Probe their past by learning how their family of origin has impacted their lives.

Revisit their values by clearly defining them and living them out when pressured to veer off course.

Expose their triangles by understanding how they relate in their current relationships and by staying separate yet connected to others while not trying to force them to change.

Search for their gaps by becoming aware of the people-pleasing traps into which they fall.

Engage their dissidents and critics by keeping a calm, connected presence with them.

Nurture their soul through Christ-centered mindfulness.

Tame their reactivity by moderating their reactions through Spirit-directed thoughtfulness.

Growing into a mature PRESENT leader does not come easily nor does it come quickly. Yet becoming a more PRESENT leader will satisfy your heart, honor the Lord and maximize your leadership influence. In the remainder of the book, I will suggest practical and specific ways that can help you develop into such a leader. I hope as you continue to read you'll do so with an open mind rather than with a Semmelweis reflex like that of the proud doctors who refused to wash their hands to save lives, considering that practice to be beneath them. If you sense that people pleasing might be hindering your leadership, let God speak to your heart and guide you to appropriate change.

Ben Arment's Take

Ben Arment, the uber-creative guy who founded the Story Conference and Dream Year (benarment.com), offers these wise words about people pleasing.

> Focus on your life's work, not your job's work. When you see your role in the context of a lifetime, you stop worrying about the short-term repercussions of acting courageously. People's opinions matter less. Their criticism doesn't sting so badly. You've got the long view, which may keep other people guessing, but it's what matters most and keeps you in the game.

YOUR TAKE

- How would your closest friend rate your emotional maturity?
- Think about the avocado metaphor. How solid is your inner core?

SECTION II

The Solution

4

PROBE YOUR PAST

> *Those who cannot remember the past*
> *are condemned to repeat it.*
>
> GEORGE SANTANYA, PHILOSOPHER

HE WAS JUST CURIOUS like all little boys his age. He couldn't fathom what his tiny hands were about to cause. He reached up to grasp the handle, and a moment later his mother heard a wrenching cry that would haunt her for years.

Built around corn and tobacco fields, Oak Park, Georgia, was not much of a town. At the only stop sign, a small feed store sat on one corner and a gas station that doubled as a general store sat on the other. Oak Park was so remote that nobody owned a phone. If you needed to make a phone call, you'd have to use the only one in town, at the general store.

Gertrude, a diminutive, wiry woman less than five feet tall had lived in Oak Park her entire life. With her husband, Mansfield, she had two boys and one girl: Woodrow, Lee and Cassie Doris. Their farm included several acres of corn, a few acres of tobacco, a hen house and some pear trees. Although they were dirt poor, Gertrude always seemed to be able to put food on the table.

Somehow she had come across a book on how to be a midwife. After successfully delivering a few babies, news of her skills spread until she became the unofficial doctor in Oak Park. If you ever got sick, you'd call Gertrude, because the nearest real doctor lived a few hours away in Vidalia. No matter who called, she'd faithfully show up and use her home remedies to help as best she could.

One day as Gertrude was canning snap beans, a neighbor rushed into her house and breathlessly yelled, "Gertrude, Gertrude. Please come! Please come! It's little Jimmy!" Without asking for details, she grabbed the flour sack filled with her home remedies and followed her friend's horse in an old, two-horse wagon.

The trip took about ten minutes. Just a brief explanation from her friend en route was all Gertrude needed to know. Little Jimmy probably wouldn't make it.

They pulled up to the old farmhouse, and already scores of family and friends were milling about. She ran in and there lay three-year-old Jimmy, his raspy breathing barely keeping his little body alive.

It could have been dried navy beans soaking in cold water. Or it could have be those same beans in a boiling cauldron. In Jimmy's case, it was the latter. Out of curiosity he had simply reached up and grabbed the pot handle. The water cascaded over his head, burning 75 percent of his body.

Gertrude kneeled down by Jimmy, breathed a short prayer and took out some ointment. She gently spread it on his red cheeks, knowing it wouldn't save him, yet she hoped it might ease his pain a bit. She knew, however, what his labored breathing meant. An hour later Jimmy's spirit left this earth. Tears flowed freely that day in Oak Park.

Although Gertrude's job was technically done, she stayed. She stayed to help prepare the little boy's body for burial. In those days, small towns didn't have funeral homes. The deceased family performed everything funeral homes do today.

Gertrude lingered until evening as she helped with the funeral preparations. She cleaned his lifeless body and dressed him in his Sunday best. The mom was grateful for her help, but noticed something puzzling about Gertrude. She hadn't shed a tear. So she asked, "Gertrude, aren't you grieving?"

"Yes. I grieve with you," she said, "but my tears are on the inside."

....

I sat misty-eyed on the ottoman, listening to my mother tell me this story about Gertrude, her mother, whom I called Granny. I still recall many fond memories of our visits to her farmhouse in Oak Park until she died when I was twelve. This story increased my respect for her.

My mom had not yet finished telling the story, though. She added one final statement that struck a deep chord in my soul. She said, "I'm like that too. I keep my emotions inside." When she said those words, I silently voiced these words to myself: *Why, I'm like that too. That's why I keep my emotions inside.*

This crucial insight helped me finally see a major influence behind one of the greatest struggles in my life, emotional vulnerability. Through the years, some have described me as a person who doesn't easily emotionally connect to others. Although I had tried to be more vulnerable, I still found it difficult. I had always wondered why it was so hard. Then when I heard my mom tell this story about how she and her mother had struggled with their emotional vulnerability, it shed light on why I, too, was like that. And I felt a new freedom inside.

This story illustrates how traits from prior generations can profoundly impact us. I never would have heard this story or felt its positive impact had I not intentionally asked my mom to tell me about her childhood. The training I had recently received in Bowen Family Systems had prompted me to visit my parents to learn about their pasts. Family systems theory teaches that we bring issues from previous generations, both good and bad, into our lives. For spiritual leaders, those issues affect how we lead.

A good metaphor for how our past still influences our present is "an infinitely long collapsing telescope in which each generation overlaps and to some extent shapes the next 'cylinder of time.'"[1] We are affected by the emotional influences from our past, and I believe the Bible's genealogical lists reflect this. The more we learn about generational influences the better we can free ourselves from their unhealthy patterns, especially people pleasing, because it often finds its roots in prior generations. As we learn about our family's past, we can also embrace and celebrate the healthy influences.

Chapter snapshot: Probe your past. This chapter describes how our family of origin influences our pleaser tendencies. It explains what a family diagram is as well as how to create one to understand how your family dynamics pass down into future generations (and into your leadership). Just as our biological family embodies certain pleaser tendencies, our church family does as well. I'll also explain how boards and staff are influenced by their past and how pastors can better equip themselves to manage conflict and tension with them when it arises.

GENERATIONAL INFLUENCE IN THE BIBLE

Pastor-author Pete Scazzero points out in his book *Emotionally Healthy Spirituality* that when the Bible speaks about family, it includes our extended families to three and four generations past.[2] Dysfunctional patterns from prior generations often show up in biblical characters' lives, just as a lack of emotional vulnerability in my prior generations showed up in me. This passage illustrates this principle.

> You shall not make for yourself an idol in the form of any-
> thing in heaven above or on the earth beneath or in the
> waters below. You shall not bow down to them or worship
> them; for I, the LORD your God, am a jealous God, punishing
> the children for the sin of the fathers to the third and fourth
> generation of those who hate me, but showing love to a
> thousand [generations] of those who love me and keep my
> commandments. (Ex 20:4-6)

This doesn't mean that God punishes children because of a father's or a grandfather's sins. Rather it speaks to how generational sin
and dysfunction in the family dynamic often passes down the family
tree. A baby born to an alcoholic mother will be more prone to
misuse alcohol than one born to a nonalcoholic mom. Likewise, a
son will more likely to struggle with anger if his dad is a rage-aholic.

The following biblical examples illustrate generational influence:

- Lying, favoritism, cutting off relationships and a lack of intimacy
  are passed down through Abraham, Isaac and Jacob.

- The Bible often describes the kings of Israel as doing evil or good,
  following in the footsteps of their fathers, who did the same.

- King David, even though called a man after God's own heart,
  lusted and committed adultery with Bathsheba. His son Amnon's lust for and rape of his stepsister Tamar mirrors David's
  behavior (2 Sam 13).

- David's murder of Bathsheba's husband reflected in his son Absalom's execution of his stepbrother Amnon (2 Sam 11; 13).

Family patterns from our past clearly play out in our lives and
in our families, including people-pleasing patterns. Often we unconsciously follow these hidden yet powerful scripts that influence
our self-esteem, our personal convictions, the way we lead and
how we relate to others.

How can we stop these cycles, these hidden scripts contrary to Christ-honored living and leading? For a Christian, the Lord can end these cycles, but only if we cooperate with him and ferret out these patterns, including people pleasing. When we come to Christ, he gives us a new nature, a new family, a new heart, new desires and new resources to deal with life's challenges. However, most ingrained patterns don't immediately disappear when we come to faith. It takes time, self-awareness, hard work and the Holy Spirit to weaken such patterns. We must go back to reconnect with and learn from our families of origin to see how these dynamics play out in our lives today. Creating a family diagram, also called a genogram, can help that process.

In fact, counselors who extensively use family systems concepts have found that the very act of trying to reconnect, especially if you've cut off relationships or distanced yourself from siblings or parents, often brings healing. I'm not suggesting you put yourself in harm's way if you come from an abusive family. I'm not saying this process comes easily, especially if you don't have a good relationship with your parents or if they are no longer alive. And I'm not promising instant results. I am saying, however, that if you take some effort to look back, you will be able to move forward in fresh ways. Scazzero and his wife, Geri, have helped hundreds of people take that look back and have seen much fruit as a result. He captures the essence of probing your past in this pithy statement: "You must go back in order to go forward."[3]

In fact we can trace many of our people-pleasing tendencies to influences from our families of origin. The following family dysfunctions often contribute to people-pleasing patterns.

- Perfectionistic parents who set the bars so high that their children seldom received affirmation and love from them. Affirmation in these families was conditional. Nagging "oughts" and "shoulds" still whisper in the minds of those children long into adulthood.

- Being super nice or compliant garnered approval from parents. Pastors who came from these homes subconsciously think that being nice in their churches will likewise make people happy.

- Growing up in a home where one or both parents were alcoholics.

- Having parents who excessively doted on their children or extravagantly praised them.

Although probing our past may surface some of these unhealthy patterns, it should also remind us of the good things that flow from one generation into the next. It's not just about finding unhealthy patterns, but also about discovering and celebrating healthy emotional and relational patterns.

I've seen this in my life as I've listened to my parents' stories. For example, I have a strong sense of justice. When I learn that someone has been slighted because of her age, color or socioeconomic background, it angers me and prompts me to action. Fortunately my parents raised my sister and me to look beyond skin color and other external traits in others. But that perspective goes back even further. My dad often told me that one of his best childhood friends was black. And on one visit home, Dad told me the following amazing story.

In the late 1800s, a relative on my dad's side of the family took a trip to Georgia. This was at the height of slavery in the United States. On his trip he passed through a small town in south Georgia (not Oak Park). When he arrived, he noticed a commotion in the town square. He got closer to see what was going on. When he saw what caused the commotion, he became incensed. Slaves were being sold, and he had never seen a slave auction before.

At that moment a young woman was being placed on the auction block. Almost without a thought, he bid the highest amount and bought her. He immediately gave her total freedom. She was so touched that she asked if he would allow her to work in his household. He hired her, and she faithfully worked for him for many years.

As I heard my dad tell me this story, I realized that my sense of justice is a gift that my family has passed down to me. I hope I perpetuate that same sense of justice. I think I see it in my oldest daughter.

Appeasement made one pastor feel like a fake

I brought a list of expectations to the church staff that I wanted to introduce and secure their agreement to subscribe to. These expectations included issues regarding their moral behavior and an expectation that they be worshiping somewhere at a local church and giving, serving and growing in their faith. There was great resistance to these, and I have backed down from them to placate the staff. Doing so makes me feel somewhat fraudulent, as we ask these things of the members but don't feel we can ask them of people who are receiving a paycheck from the church.

TIPS FOR CREATING YOUR FAMILY DIAGRAM

Creating your own family diagram takes time, but it is worth it. First, if your parents are living, schedule a time to see them. Just visit and ask questions about their pasts. When I visited my parents to learn their stories, they were delighted to share them. My dad had even collected several letters from his grandmother and had compiled some family genealogy information. They both remarked how pleased they were that I wanted to know their stories. If your parents aren't alive, reach out to other relatives that may have known your parents or grandparents. Include your brothers and sisters as well in your quest to learn from your past.

I realize this process may seem daunting to some. But even if you don't complete the full process I recommend, you'll find that a couple of hours thinking about your family influences will benefit you. Family systems expert Margaret Marcuson writes, "The more we learn about our family story, the more we learn about ourselves."[4]

You may question the usefulness of this exercise, especially if you've experienced tension with your extended family. Ron Richardson, a pastoral counselor who has written extensively about how our family system applies to our ministry setting, addresses that concern:

> Most of us hesitate to do this. We fear getting trapped or swallowed up in that family system. The more resistant people are to doing family work, the more likely they are to be emotionally trapped in that system, even while keeping their distance. The fact is that we don't grow up and become mature by staying away from those people. We gain emotional separation and maturity by getting closer to them and working at being a self in their presence.[5]

Don't limit your inquisitiveness to a single visit. Make it an ongoing experience. On subsequent visits to my parents' home, I continue to ask them about their life stories.

As you begin to collect your stories, create a visual representation of them with a family diagram. Below you will find a very simple genogram of my family to give you an idea what one looks like. (You can find many more examples on the web.) Below it, I've included a chart that shows the basic symbols to use when you create yours. If you want a fuller explanation, the booklet *A Family Genogram Workbook* by Israel Galindo, Elaine Boomer and Don Reagan goes into depth on how to make one. You may even want to create your diagram with one of many genogram computer programs available.

You'll create your diagram in three phases. First, gather your stories as I described above. Use the standard who, what, where,

My Family Diagram

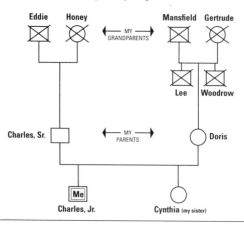

Figure 4.1.

You can refer to the key on this page as you develop your genogram. Be consistent in the use of symbols so that your genogram will be easy to interpret.

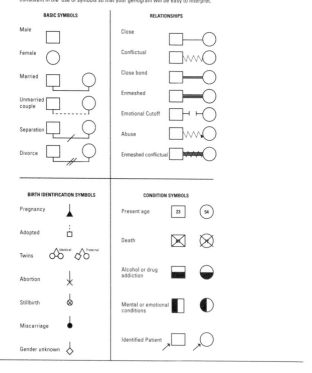

Figure 4.2.

when and why questions. Second, group your insights into categories. These questions will help:

- What effect did birth order have on your family?
- How did your family handle anger and conflict?
- Are there any family secrets or skeletons?
- How did your family view your role? What role do you believe you played?
- If your family has a family motto, what's behind it?
- How do you see family patterns playing out in your ministry today (open, closed, reactionary, distancing and so on)?
- How did your family handle crises and losses?
- How did your parents relate to each other and to their siblings and parents?
- Do any addictions run in your family?
- How did your family handle spirituality? Money? Holidays? Relationships with extended family members?
- What early childhood events taught you about leadership? Did family members see leadership qualities in you as a young person? What were those qualities?

Now that you've gathered your stories and answered several key questions, draw your diagram. Using the symbols for close, conflictual, enmeshed, cut off and so on, show how key members related to each other. Then look for core themes.

As you create your diagram, add names, birth and death years, and brief notes that describe each person. Also note watershed events in the family (miscarriages, major family crisis, deaths, world events and so on). If you expand your genogram to your grandparents (or even great-grandparents), you should have enough information to notice trends and repeating patterns.

Creating your family diagram won't make unhealthy patterns magically disappear, but it will give you fresh insight about yourself. Over time, painful life experiences will continue to lose their sting. Understanding these patterns will help you begin to change the unhealthy ones that influence how you relate to your board, your staff, your family and your critics.

Keep in mind that I don't mean to imply that this discovery process is a way for you to fix family problems. That's not the goal. Rather, by understanding more about yourself, you'll be able to see your people pleasing and other unhealthy patterns—and with the Spirit's help, change them.

TIPS ON MAPPING YOUR CHURCH

A family diagram yields much insight into how we personally function, relate and lead. You can also create a genogram of your church to learn how people have perpetuated unhealthy patterns there. I wish I had known about family diagrams before I began to pastor. If I had seen how dysfunctional batons pass from one leader or significant stakeholder to the next, I could have avoided a lot of grief—or least prepared myself to handle those issues better.

I recall one church I served where the founding pastor had been a father figure to many of the early members. He was "larger than life" from both the stage and in one-on-one relationships. Because many of the old-timers had come to faith through his ministry, most had never seen any other pastor lead. He had become close friends with many of the stakeholders, making himself available to them 24-7. The father figure he played loomed large.

When I arrived as senior pastor, my leadership style was not to give people 24-7 availability, except in emergencies, because I'd soon burn out if I did. I was also a ready-aim-fire leader, whereas he was known as a fire-fire-fire leader.

After about a year, I began to sense a weird vibe from some of the stakeholder leaders. It seemed that I couldn't please them, no matter what I did. I felt befuddled. But as a clearer picture of the previous pastor emerged, I began to understand what fueled this tension. I realized that some leaders wanted the best parts of him—in me. They wanted a father figure who was available 24-7. One leader even confessed to me that he expected me to be a father to him. They also loved his larger-than-life dreams that seemed to come "straight from the Holy Spirit." It excited them, and many felt that church should be perpetually exciting. My vision, however, came more slowly through a more deliberate and thoughtful process, definitely not eliciting as much initial excitement as his did.

They had transferred the idealized former pastor's strengths onto me, and I had failed to meet those expectations. Edwin Friedman captured this transference when he noted, "Institutions . . . tend to institutionalize the pathology, or the genius, of the founding families."[6]

This founding pastor had left under difficult circumstances. As a result I also bumped into another unspoken script: a fear and distrust of strong pastoral leadership among some stakeholder leaders. Had I known how churches, like families, pass down dysfunctions, I could have better navigated those bumps.

If you're a senior pastor, I encourage you to probe your church's past to learn the hidden scripts against which you may be bumping. Take some key leaders and long-term members out to lunch and ask about the church's history. Listen especially to the stories from the old-timers. The more you learn about your church's past, the better you'll respond to its dysfunctions. I've listed some questions below that you might ask these leaders.

- What significant events, both successes and traumas, have marked your church's history?
- How has your church responded to traumas and crises?
- What problems seem to recur in your church?
- Does your church have any deep, dark secrets?

- How did the church begin? Was it from a church split? Was it a plant from another church?

- Are relatives of the founding families still in the church? Are some of the founding members still in places of influence?

- What stories of God's moving do people still tell?

- How long have pastors stayed? What were the circumstances behind their departures? How were their departures handled? How do people talk about the prior pastors?

- Is there an ongoing pattern of firing staff?

- Have any recurring sins persisted in staff or key leaders (sexual immorality, financial malfeasance, gossip and so on)?

You're likely to find some repeating patterns. Simply knowing what you're up against and paying attention to these multigenerational dynamics can give you a head start in dealing with the patterns. While acknowledging the past, you can more wisely lead your church into the future, knowing that these past patterns still play a part in the present. Quoting Scazzero again, "To go forward, you must go back."

Figure 4.3 is a fictional example of how someone might loosely

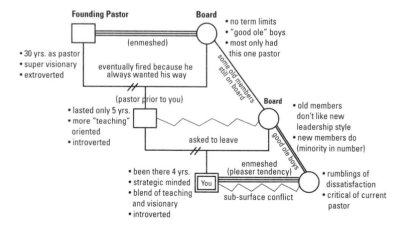

Figure 4.3.

diagram a church's dynamics going back several years (or several pastors).

A FINAL NOTE

Keep in mind that probing your past is not about pointing out what's wrong in your church or your parents. It's not about living in the past. It's not about trying to change your family members or pointing out their flaws. Rather, it's learning about your family (or church) so you can become a healthier you and a healthier leader so that you in turn can pass down on to the next generation many good gifts that will build the kingdom of God.

DAN REILAND'S TAKE

Dan Reiland serves as executive pastor of 12Stone Church outside Atlanta, one of the country's fastest-growing churches. He has also authored the book *Amplified Leadership* (danreiland.com). Here's his insight on people pleasing:

> People like you best when you are yourself. Relax, be you. Not everyone will like you, but they like you best when you are the real you, because they can sense your heart and connect with you. Remember, while you lie awake at night worried about what they think, they are snoring! Get some rest and lead from the real you.

YOUR TAKE

- When you think about delving into your past and into how it influences your leadership, what kinds of feelings surface?

- What could those feelings be telling you?

The Search Within

REVISIT YOUR VALUES

> I was learning the hard way that the gospel alone
> can free us from our addiction to being liked—
> that Jesus measured up for us so that we wouldn't
> have to live under the enslaving pressure
> of measuring up for others.
>
> TULLIAN TCHIVIDJIAN,
> PASTOR AND GRANDSON OF BILLY GRAHAM

WITH A CADENCE THAT WOULD have fit an execution, the drums set the tone for the humiliation that was to follow. Set in post–Civil War times, the hewn log walls of the old fort surrounded the two lines of uniformed soldiers as they stood motionless behind the flagpole. Six soldiers, two by two, marched parallel to the lines, stopped and performed a sharp right face. The lead soldier in this group of six, Jason McCord, a West Point graduate, stood a head taller than the others. His steely gaze fixed straight ahead as he stood at attention.

With disdain, his commander stepped up to him, snatched Mc-Cord's hat off and tossed it aside. With his left hand he reached above McCord's left shoulder and tore off his insignia, repeating the same with his right insignia. With disgust he then ripped his uniform's buttons off, one by one. And in one final act of ignominy, he jerked the saber off McCord's side. Stepping back with a contemptuous flair, he pulled it from its sheath, cast one last sneering glance at him and snapped the sword in two over his knee. The sound of it cracking reverberated throughout the fort. After he dropped the pointed piece in the dust, he tossed the handled piece out the fort's open doors.

He stepped aside as McCord stoically walked out of the fort. Two soldiers shut the gate behind him. McCord picked up his broken sabre, and as he stared at it he pondered his fate. He realized what lay ahead: a life in the shadow of shame from a false accusation.

Months prior, McCord's mentor, General James Reed, along with McCord and a unit of thirty-one men, had been sent on a peace mission to the Apache Nation at Bitter Creek. Unfortunately, in an attack like that at Little Big Horn, renegade Indians called dog soldiers had overwhelmed the soldiers. As the attack began, McCord realized that the general's mental deterioration had left him unfit to lead, so he released him of his command.

Every soldier died in that attack but McCord, who was left for dead. In a coma for ten days, he recovered but was later court-martialed. The charge? Desertion. Being the lone survivor, the authorities assumed he had fled the battle to save himself.

After his cashiering (the process described above), he traveled west and became a nomad, drifting from one job to the next. It seemed that everywhere he went his reputation preceded him; he was branded a coward who abandoned his fellow soldiers to save his own skin. In silence he suffered from both overt and covert attacks from others.

However, many who initially hated him ended up admiring him. The accusation of cowardice simply didn't match his behavior. In fact, McCord's actions toward them actually inspired many to do the right thing when they faced difficult decisions. His words and deeds, contrary to his reputation, gave them strength and courage to do that right thing. Most now saw him as a man of integrity and convictions, nothing like the label pinned on him.

Far from being a coward, McCord was indeed a man of deep principle and conviction. In his court-martial he pleaded innocent but refused to testify in his own defense. He held a secret that would have exonerated him. What was his secret? Subsequent to his court-martial, he discovered that a widow of the third in command at Bitter Creek had received several letters from her husband before his death that also questioned General Reid's mental stability. They would have been enough for a retrial and exoneration.

Yet McCord had convinced the widow to burn the letters. Why? He wanted to protect the memory of General Reid and to protect the peace treaty made with the Indians. He believed that if Washington knew what had really happened on that peace mission, the politicians would nullify the treaty and resume war with the Apaches.

Thus was the storyline of the 1960s TV show *Branded*, starring Chuck Connors. Each episode began with the same trailer showing McCord's cashiering that I described above. A cowboy ballad played behind it (view the YouTube trailer to get the full effect). The lyrics posed the question "What do you do with the rest of your life when you're falsely accused of not being a person of character?"

For the two seasons the show ran, each episode centered on a life situation where McCord answered that question in this way: You simply live out your true character, and your actions will reveal the true you. Jason McCord, as played by Chuck Connors, modeled the essence of this chapter. Great leaders counter people pleasing by living from their convictions and values.

Chapter snapshot: Revisit your values. In this chapter I explain that we must clarify and anchor our core values and convictions to best counter unhealthy approval-seeking tendencies. The chapter will describe how clearly rooted convictions help us navigate the minefields of leadership, much like a ship's captain depends on a gyrocompass to guide his ship rather than trust a simple compass. Few external forces can force a gyrocompass to give false readings (and thus cause a ship to veer off course), whereas a small magnet can easily cause a compass needle to point the wrong way.

John Ortberg, one of today's most insightful authors, captures approval addiction with these words:

> Some people live in bondage to what others think of them. The addiction takes many forms. If we find ourselves often getting hurt by what others say about us, by people expressing other than glowing opinions about us, we probably have it. If we habitually compare ourselves with other people, if we find ourselves getting competitive in the most ordinary situations, we probably have it. If we live with a nagging sense that we aren't important enough or special enough, or we get envious of another's success, we probably have it. If we keep trying to impress important people, we probably have it. If we are worried that someone might think ill of us should he or she find out we are an approval addict, we probably are.[1]

The book of Daniel describes four men whose lives modeled the opposite of what Ortberg describes. Historically, the Babylonian king Nebuchadnezzar would conquer other lands and capture the most promising and talented young men. He'd then train them in the culture and eventually press them into service. When he invaded Israel, the Scripture tells us that four teenaged boys stood

out: Daniel, Hananiah, Mishael and Azariah, whose names Nebuchadnezzar changed to Belteshazzar, Shadrach, Meshach and
Abednego. For the next three years he indoctrinated them into
pagan Babylonian culture.

The book describes several times when these young men could
have compromised their values, yet didn't:

- Daniel's refusal to break faith with God by eating food and wine
  used in pagan sacrifices (Dan 1)

- Shadrach, Meshach and Abednego's refusal to bow down and
  worship the king's statue, resulting in their being thrown in an
  executioner's furnace to be burned, yet miraculously being
  rescued (Dan 3)

- Daniel's refusal in his later years to obey a subsequent king's
  order that everyone should worship the pagan gods for thirty
  days, resulting in his being thrown into the lion's den for execution, yet also being miraculously rescued (Dan 6)

What kept these men from compromising, giving in, cutting
corners, spinning the truth or hedging? Why did they refuse the
path of least resistance that would have been to their immediate
benefit? What enabled them to resist compromise when faced
with cultural pressures to do so? They had a true north, a strong
moral compass—deeply ingrained values and convictions from
which they would not depart. Christian leaders need the same to
lead in ministry environments that often press us to compromise
our vision and values in order to make people happy and get them
to like us.

WHAT ARE YOUR VALUES?

Do this quick exercise right now. In the box below, write down your
answer to this question: What core values and convictions guide
your life and ministry? If you haven't memorized them, go to the
document on your computer or in a file where you've listed them.

Commitment

Hard work

Trustworthiness

Connection

Commitment

trustworthy

team player

honesty

Were you able to easily write them down? Were they fuzzy or hard to locate? Or was this the first time you've considered what they were? When I say values, I don't mean the essential values every believer should embrace, like keeping the Ten Commandments, obeying the Golden Rule or living out Jesus' great command and Great Commission. Rather I'm speaking about more nuanced ones that capture the essence of the real you.

Daniel and his friends lived these kinds of values. These values so infuse our soul that nothing external can cause us to compromise them. Granted, they might be aspirational, ones not yet fully developed. Nevertheless, they describe the authentic, Christ-honoring you to which you aspire.

It's like the difference between a compass and a gyrocompass. A compass points to true north because it relies on magnetic north—unless, that is, you bring a magnet close to it. Even a small magnet can cause a compass to give wrong directions. A magnet external to it affects the north arrow so that it gives a false reading. Metaphorically, the magnet makes it compromise. For some so-called values, all it takes is criticism or the oppositional voice of a significant board member (an external force) to cause a leader to compromise.

Samson was a leader with "compass" values. As a Nazarite, he had made a vow (swore to a list of "values") to avoid certain behaviors. Usually in that day a person's joy and a desire to set himself apart for God prompted such a vow. In his case, however, it was prophesied that he would be a Nazarite from birth (Judg 13:5). But from the very beginning Samson found it difficult to live up to those values. He became involved with three different Philistine women, one ultimately leading to his downfall.

Gary McIntosh and Samuel Rima write, "Samson had a deep need to please others. It was very hard for him to disappoint anyone. In fact it was nearly impossible for him to say 'No' even when saying yes was in his best interest and ultimately was self-destructive."[2] When something (or someone) exerted pressure on his values, his compass didn't keep him fixed on his true north.

People pleasing led to putting more work on one pastor's plate

As an associate pastor, part of my job means deferring to our senior pastor. There have been times when I have appeased him rather than trying really hard to help him understand why I disagreed with a decision he made. I then have invested an inordinate amount of time and energy trying to make the decision work. This has meant that I didn't do some things that might have been more fruitful. And fruitless work eventually disheartens me.

Approval-motivated leadership left another pastor with hollow victories

When I appease, I question my own strength as a leader and as a Christian. I also doubt my capacity for the kind of leadership I respect in others. While I am having "success," it rarely feels like a victory to me.

TRUE NORTH VALUES AND HOW THEY HELP

In contrast to a compass, a gyrocompass models the nuanced values I'm writing about. For navigation, ships use gyrocompasses, devices that combine a compass with a gyroscope. They find true north from the Earth's rotation, which is navigationally more useful than magnetic north. Additionally, a gyrocompass's strength lies in its ability to keep true north even if magnetic material is placed near it.

In a parallel way, our deeply imbedded values are not those we are glib about. Rather, they stand up under severe external or internal circumstances that would tempt us to compromise. Daniel and his three friends, as well as Jason McCord as depicted in *Branded*, modeled such values.

When our church faces a crisis, our anxiety rises and we feel pressure to find answers quickly. These pressures can come from staff, board members, declining offerings or attendance, or squeaky wheels in the church. Our anxiety rises too, and often we lead out of our emotions by reacting to the situation, rather than by thoughtfully leading from our deep values. When we're unclear about these values, we often seek a quick fix or a short-term solution to allay the anxiety. But when we're clear and convinced about our core values, they help define, protect and guide us. Values clarity helps us keep our true north when we're coerced to give in to please others or otherwise compromise.

Such values act much like a guardian for our hearts, as seen in Proverbs 4:23: "Above all else, guard your heart, for it is the wellspring of life." They help us take clear positions when facing challenge and uncertainty. They help us keep connected to relationships when we're tempted to cut others off (see chapter 8) or lose our identities by fusing with others (see chapter 7). Gyrocompass values give us courage to say what we believe and what others can expect from us without trying to change those who may oppose us. Clear values help us embody what one of my teachers on family systems, Dr. Roberta Gilbert, would describe as "responsible responsibility."

Dr. Lawrence Matthews, a pastor for forty-two years and a powerful voice for applying family systems to ministry, explains the importance of clarifying such values. He equates these values with defining your self.

> To define self is to give expression to the thoughts, values and goals one holds dear. It includes taking stands. To use biblical language, it is self-revelation. I have come to understand this as one of my major tasks as a pastor. My responsibility is to get clear about what I think and believe and communicate those thoughts and beliefs in words and actions—not to get others straight about what they should think and believe.[3]

My family systems coach, Dr. Scotty Hargrove, helped me see the importance of clear values. I once faced an issue about office hours with a staff person who would sometimes emotionally react to me. It was very draining. I needed to confront him about this issue, and my anxiety went sky high when I thought about it. Scotty suggested that to deal with my anxiety about this situation, I needed to clarify my values.

He asked, "What are your core values in this situation?" As I pondered his question, I realized my angst came from two competing values. On the one hand, I wanted to be fair to all my staff and allow flexibility based on individual personality and gifts. On the other hand, I had to keep in mind the church's need for a certain performance level. I needed to clarify my limits. Where was my comfort range in allowing staff flexibility? I needed to operationalize that comfort level.

When I began to clarify those values, my anxiety dropped, because I no longer focused on the staff person's emotional reactivity. Rather, I was able to clearly think through how to balance equal treatment of all staff with reasonable performance expectations the church needed. So values clarity helped me maintain objectivity and avoid needless anxiety.

From the almost one hundred pages of personal stories about pastors who people pleased, I've excerpted the two stories below that show what happens when we aren't clear about our gyro-compass values.

> People want me to preach a certain way that I don't think is biblical or fits me. I try to appease them by doing some of what they want, but my whole heart is not behind it. They are not open to discussing it in a rational way, so I feel backed into a corner. They are unhappy with me, and I am unhappy with the pressure being put on me.

> I did not share with the senior pastor when he was failing to lead the staff, out of fear of hurting his feelings. Then when it all boiled over and everyone on the staff shared how hurt they had been, I agreed with them. The pastor then turned on me and called me disloyal. It created such an unhappy environment that I had to resign from leading the youth ministry.

What Gyrocompass Values Look Like

If these gyrocompass values are so essential, how do we determine them and what do they look like? In 2012 a movie by Steven Spielberg about Abraham Lincoln's life premiered. At that time I also read a great article on Lincoln's character by Mark Crowley.[4] His article lists several attributes that would fit gyrocompass values. I've summarized some of his thoughts on Lincoln by reframing them as possible value statements.

- *I will learn through loss.* He grew up in abject poverty, his mother died when he was nine and he witnessed the death of both his infant brother and his older sister.

- *I will become a lifelong learner.* Entirely self-taught, he was seldom seen without a book under his arm.

- *I will live out my divine purpose.* He believed he was destined to engrave his name on history.

- *I won't bury my adversaries.* He didn't vilify his opponents; he even appointed to his cabinet three men he defeated for the Republican presidential nomination.

- *I will develop my ability to empathize.* He had a keen ability to empathize with others at a heart level.

- *I will learn to connect with people's hearts when I communicate.* He moved people through his speeches and writing with his storytelling ability, his humanness and his kindness. One of his greatest quotes embodies this quality: "In order to win a man to your cause, you must first reach his heart, the great high road to his reason."

- *I will truly care about people.* People knew he cared about others, evidenced by his encouraging words and his thoughtful behavior toward them.

As another example, I've included my gyrocompass values below. As I developed mine, I realize that I must constantly keep them in front of me so that the Lord can remind me about them and drive them deeper into my soul. It's important to review them regularly, because they're a work in progress; God can add one to your list, tweak existing ones and remind you which ones need shoring up. There's no right way to write them, and keep in mind that a values list differs from a mission or vision statement.

You may or may not want to tie specific Scriptures to your list. Although I don't use many Scriptures below, I've filled my personal mission statement with Bible verses.

God: Seek to please him in all that I do.

Thinking: Pay attention to my thoughts.
- I will not default to worst-case scenario thinking.
- I will check out my thinking before acting on it.
- I will not assume the worst when in the dark.
- I will not connect dots when I have no evidence to do so.

- I will monitor my anxiety.

Speech: Say what I mean and mean what I say, all with grace.

Integrity: Live in such a way that I can authentically say, "Watch me and do what I do."

- Integrity both inside and out
- Good example for my family and others

Self-care: Take care of myself.

- Body care
- Process my emotional pain
- Weekly sabbath rest
- Balance (Lk 2:52)

Growth: Never stop learning.

- Stimulate my mind with good books and exposure to others who will stretch me.
- Learn from adversity.
- Keep resilient in the face of criticism, difficulty and hardship.

Relationships: Resist cutoff.

- Calmly connect with critics and troublemakers.
- Refuse to avoid difficult people.
- Give others the benefit of the doubt.

Reactivity: Manage it.

- I will think before I speak.
- I will stay vigilant when I'm tempted to be defensive.

Listening: Seek understanding before being understood.

Tips for Creating Your Own Gyrocompass Values

The following exercises can help you determine your gyrocompass values. I believe they're so crucial that we must invest significant time and energy to discern them. I've listed them below as steps. I also recommend a great tool, a book called *Do More Great Work: Stop the Busywork, Start the Work That Matters* by Michael Bungay Stanier. He goes deep on some of the steps I recommend below. Before you actual begin the process, it's important to prepare in these ways:

- Ask a few close friends, coworkers and/or family members to write their response to this question: *In your experience with me, what do you see are my core strengths, passions, gifts and competencies?*

- Block out half a day for a mini-retreat alone. Better yet, schedule an overnight retreat for even more time to discern your values. Take your Bible, pen, paper and computer. Also take any personality or leadership inventories you have taken, as well as the above feedback from your friends and family.

- Recruit two or three prayer partners who will pray for you as you seek God's will about your values.

At your discernment retreat, use the eight steps below. If you've scheduled a half-day, you can plan for about thirty minutes for each part. If you've scheduled an overnight retreat, consider taking an hour or so for each part. The goal for each step is to create a list of ten or fewer themes, words or concepts for each category. Then you'll combine them into your final list.

1. *Delights*. Ask yourself, "What truly delights me? What do I love doing? What do I do that I enjoy so much that I seem to lose track of time when I do it?" Write down fewer than ten thoughts and ideas on a piece of paper.

2. *Past*. Think over your past. Write down answers to these questions:

- When you were a kid, what was fun? Where did you get your joy? What did you like doing more than anything else? What themes do you see emerging?

- Move now to high school and then to college, and ask the same questions.

- Combine your themes into a list of no more than ten.

3. *Peak performance.* Think about when you are at your best. Write down your answers to these questions.

   - Think of peak moments in your life or career, those moments when you feel that you did your very best work or made your greatest contribution or difference. Why were those peak moments? What was true about you? What was ignited in your soul? Do you see any themes emerging?

   - Last week, when were you at your best? Why?

   - Last month, when were you at your best? Why?

   - Last year, when were you at your best? Why?

   - Approach this from the opposite direction: when are you not at your best?

   - List words that describe you when you were at your best in your peak moments from your exercises above. List no more than twenty. Now narrow that list to no more than ten. Play with those words a while until you get colorful, descriptive words that describe you when you are at your best.

4. *Heroes.* Think of those in your past or present that you'd consider your heroes. What qualities about them prompted you to put them on your list? Narrow those qualities down to fewer than ten.

5. *Input from others.* Look at the answers to the questions you posed to your coworkers, friends and family. Make a list of themes, fewer than ten, that stand out among their comments.

6. *Scripture.* Write down the key Scriptures or Bible characters that have meant the most to you. Create a list of fewer than ten themes from those verses and characters.

7. *Inventories.* If you brought any personality inventories you've taken, make a list of ten or fewer themes you see from them.

8. *Values list.* Finally, look at this list of words and phrases. Circle ten or fewer that resonate most with you. (Use this website as a free online tool to automate this process: oca.cce.umn.edu/ prototypes/cardsort/values.)

Accomplishment	Fast pace
Accuracy	Focus
Acknowledgment	Forward the action
Adventure	Free spirit
Aesthetics	Freedom to choose
Authenticity	Full
Balance	Fun
Beauty	Growth
Challenge	Harmony
Collaboration	Health
Community	Honesty
Compassion	Humor
Competition	Independence
Comradeship	Integrity
Connectedness	Joy
Contribution	Knowledge
Creativity	Lack of pretense
Directness	Leadership
Diversity	Lightness
Diligence	Nurturing
Elegance	Orderliness
Empowerment	Participation
Excellence	Partnership

Peace
Performance
Personal power
Physical challenge
Precision
Productivity
Recognition
Reflective
Risk taking
Romance
Safety
Self-expression

Sensitive
Service
Spirituality
Success
To be known
Tradition
Trust
Variety
Vitality
Wisdom
Zest

So, by now you have eight lists of ten or fewer terms/words per list. You've done a lot of great work. Now it's time to prayerfully begin combining the lists into one final list of ten or so words and phrases. That final list will give you a great idea about your unique gyrocompass values. Combine that final list into phrases or concepts that resonate with you. Add Scriptures if you want. Prayerfully commit to the Lord to live out these values. Ask him to help you hone them the rest of your life.

Be sure to record these in a way that will remind you to revisit them often. For example, each Monday when I look back over my prior week and plan my upcoming week, I review mine.

When pressure tempts you to compromise, to people please, to veer from your convictions or change your God-given vision, remember your gyrocompass values. Stand on them in the face of opposition and relate to others with grace and kindness. Continue to keep them before you. Be open to the Lord modifying them over time. When you do, the Rock of Ages on which you stand will be there for you as he was for Daniel, Shadrach, Meshach and Abednego.

PETE SCAZZERO'S TAKE

Pete Scazzero, author of *Emotionally Healthy Spirituality* and co-founder of Emotionally Healthy Spirituality (emotionallyhealthy .org), offers these wise words about people pleasing:

> Work on your family of origin material and how it contributes to this tendency in you. Developing a sense of self that is rooted in Christ and not in what you do or what others think is a long journey that requires courage, self-confrontation, self-awareness and self-reflection. Being stripped by God of our false selves is not for the faint of heart.

YOUR TAKE

- Without thinking much, what immediately comes to mind when you answer this question: what are my top three values?

- Did your answers surprise you?

- Ask your spouse or best friend what he or she believes are your top three core values.

When Relationships Get All Knotted Up

EXPOSE YOUR TRIANGLES

Triangles are not good or bad. . . . They are so much a fact of life that all of human society is built on triangles.

ROBERTA GILBERT

When triangles become intense, rigid and indissoluble, all the relationships involved tend to deteriorate.

DAVID W. AUGUSBURGER

He DIDN'T EXPECT WHAT HE HEARD at the personnel committee meeting. Instead of a report that a relationship had been strengthened, the opposite happened. The pointed accusation hurled from the committee chair caught him off guard. He felt like throwing up.

Mark had come to Southside Church four years prior and had inherited what he considered a competent staff. The church's constitution gave joint authority to the personnel committee and the senior pastor to hire and fire staff. And the committee had been struggling with the performance of the youth pastor, Carl, for a year. He had served at the church for twelve years and had been a driving force behind many new initiatives. But several issues had prompted committee conversations about his need to leave.

Mark felt that a gradual transition would best serve the church. In fact, Carl was planning to join a parachurch organization in twelve months, and both he and Mark wanted him to stay until that time.

Since Pastor Mark had arrived at Southside, he had tried his best to make the personnel committee happy, because they wielded so much authority. His pleaser tendencies had prompted him to keep silent on several personnel matters about which he disagreed with the committee, so as to not offend them. This issue, however, could create significant strife between him and the members.

Mark felt driven to fix the tension between the committee and Carl. So he devised a plan to have each committee member individually meet with Carl to hear his plans for a twelve-month transition. He arranged for the chairperson to meet with him first, thinking that if he could fix that relationship, the group's negative feelings toward Carl would lessen.

After a good Sunday service, Pastor Mark met with the committee. A minute into the meeting, the chairperson said he had met with Carl the day prior and had told him he should start looking for another church because he was going to be released. Mark's heart sank. He couldn't believe what he heard. He said, "You did what? You were just supposed to listen to Carl's plan for a transition, not tell him he was fired."

He shot back, "Mark, *you* were supposed to tell him that. After I found out that you *hadn't* told him, I told him." Mark went home that afternoon feeling sick to his stomach.

The next day he met with Carl, apologized for what had happened, and explained what he had hoped would have occurred. Carl appreciated Pastor Mark's empathy, and in the next several weeks they strengthened their relationship as they worked to make his transition as smooth as possible. But Mark's relationship with the personnel committee didn't fare as well. In his anger at the chairperson, he began to distance himself from the entire committee, which further increased the tension between him and the members.

This story ends with both Carl and Mark eventually leaving the church. Unbeknownst to Pastor Mark, he had interjected himself into an unhealthy relationship called an emotional triangle. Often pastors with approval-seeking tendencies place themselves in such relationships, which hinder their leadership.

> ***Chapter snapshot: Expose your triangles.*** In this chapter I un-pack the concept of emotional triangles, which often suck us into people pleasing. I show how you can map your leadership trian-gles and explain how they may contribute to unhealthy people pleasing. Biblical examples will illustrate this concept.

WHAT ARE TRIANGLES?

Triangles are the essential building blocks of relationship systems. We can't avoid them. If you spend any time with people, which pastors do (or should do), triangles form. They aren't intrinsically good or bad; they just are. I'm in a triangle with my wife and my daughter who lives at home. It's a healthy one until one of us tries to get the other one to take sides in a disagreement. Triangling is one of the major principles in family systems. So let's unpack it.

Triangles are a visual way to describe the dynamics between two people and an issue or group, or the dynamics between three people. Strained relationships between two people cause them to avoid issues by dumping burdens, shifting pain and passing anxiety to third parties. When a relationship between two people becomes too tense or uncomfortable, in order to stabilize it and decrease anxiety, another person is often triangled in. One party often seeks out someone else who will lend a sympathetic ear. This is an outflow of the principle I discussed in chapter two, homeostasis. When we feel emotionally out of balance (anxious), we take steps to get back into emotional balance. In triangling, that means bringing in a third person to shift that anxiety onto her so we can feel better.

Triangles come in many combinations. In Pastor Mark's case, his triangle was made up of him, the personnel committee and Carl. The potential triangle combinations in a church are almost endless. Here are a few common pastoral triangles:

- Pastor—church—board
- Pastor—church—issue
- Pastor—wife/husband—difficult child
- Pastor—elder—elder
- Pastor—board—church vision
- Pastor—wife/husband—church
- Pastor—staff member—staff member
- Pastor—church—denominational supervisor

After an argument with her husband, a mother can triangle in her daughter by saying, "Remember, we don't want to get your father angry." She has shifted the burden from her and her husband to the daughter and her dad. The mom may feel less tension, but not the daughter.

A father of a high school student doesn't like how the youth pastor leads the youth group, so he triangles in the senior pastor by expressing his displeasure to him. He wants the pastor to "handle" the situation. He may feel better, but the senior pastor feels worse.

The men's volunteer ministry director feels angry that the senior pastor didn't attend the annual men's camping trip, so he grumbles to the associate pastor, hoping he will relay his frustration back to the senior pastor. The director feels better, but he really doesn't solve anything. He has simply dumped on the associate pastor.

Triangling is often the way we selfishly transfer our anxiety onto others so we can feel better. In doing so, we miss opportunities to grow and to learn how to handle conflict biblically.

One pastor shared a story of how his job made him what I would call a "Triangler in Chief."

I am an associate staff minister for pastoral care. This ministry is one where "appeasing people" is a large part of the visits I make when I try to "extend" my pastor's hands. As he [the senior pastor] cannot possibly see individuals on a one-to-one basis, he assigns me to help touch every member who is homebound, hospitalized or bereaved (or a dozen other situations). Most people want to see the pastor, and a part of my ministry is to explain why he hasn't visited, without giving them the impression that he's too busy to see them personally. That's a tough one. The effect on me personally is very stressful, as I bear the effects of ministry because sometimes people make very rude remarks and spread them to others.

It's important to distinguish between a normal triangle and getting *triangled*. We'll always be in emotional triangles, because pastors must be in relationships with others to shepherd them. That's our job and what happens when we live in community. But *triangling* is an attempt by another to put us into an unhealthy position where we're tempted to try to fix the relationships between two other people. Triangling can pull a person *in* (for example, when asked, "Pastor, please meet with my husband to convince him to come to church"). Triangling can also keep a person *out* (such as when a board member talks to a disgruntled staff member without including the senior pastor with whom the staffer has the problem).

Another important distinction helps us discern when triangling is appropriate. Sometimes we need to triangle in another person when we reach an impasse in a relationship. Triangling in a counselor or wise friend for guidance in such cases is wise. Sometime we need objectivity that we can't get by ourselves. When that happens, we should not triangle to burden another with our anxiety or to sway the person to our line of thinking. Rather, we should seek another's counsel so that we can reenter the strained relationship in the most God-honoring way. I call this kind of triangle a *posture*, an appropriate choice we make for a brief time to deal with our anxiety. We also may rightfully choose a triangling posture to create needed space from another for a short time.

However, when triangling becomes habitual, it becomes unhealthy. When we regularly triangle in another to avoid working on relationships, it has become a *pattern* instead of a *posture*. Triangling as an occasional posture can foster healthy relationships, help us

When we people please, those we appease often come back to bite us.

One pastor shared, "Early in ministry I changed the midweek program for the sake of two vocal critics. I found that my instincts had been right at the beginning and eventually changed back. Far from appeasing the critics, this caused them to become openly hostile. I have learned that the loudest voice is not the most correct or important."

Another pastor described that he changed his own leadership meeting because he wanted to appease another who had a meeting at the same time. He wrote, "It wasn't long before the leader was 'slighted' by some other indication that his ministry didn't have top consideration in all decisions, and he left the church."

gain perspective and help quiet our emotions. Triangling as a pattern, however, will do the opposite, and we should avoid it.

Triangling as a pattern can hinder leadership in several ways: it can muddy decision making, inhibit healthy change management, strain team dynamics and increase relational tension. So the more we understand how triangles work, expose our own and learn to de-triangle from unhealthy ones, the more effectively we'll lead our churches. And triangles aren't a new phenomenon. They've been around since the beginning.

BIBLICAL EXAMPLES

The Bible doesn't whitewash its characters to minimize weaknesses or cover character flaws. In fact, several times it illustrates triangling. In the Genesis creation account, Adam formed the first triangle. After Adam and Eve both yielded to Satan's temptation, God asked Adam if he had eaten from the tree from which he had forbidden them to eat. Adam's response was, "The woman you put here with me—she gave me some fruit from the tree, and I ate it" (Gen 3:12). He triangled in Eve to push his guilty feelings onto her. Then when God confronted Eve, she triangled in Satan by blaming him for her disobedience (Gen 3:13).

The triangle between Paul, John Mark and Barnabas is perhaps the most prominent one in the New Testament. After Saul's conversion and his name change to Paul, many believers felt wary of him because of his history of persecuting the church. However, the relationally gifted Barnabas persuaded the apostles to accept him (Acts 9:26-27). Later Paul and Barnabas took their first missionary journey together and included John Mark.

For some unknown reason, John Mark left and returned home (Acts 13:13). Later Paul and Barnabas planned a second missionary journey, and Barnabas suggested that they include John Mark as a helper. Unfortunately, a bitter dispute erupted between the two of them about John Mark, which caused a rift between them (Acts

15:36-41). Fortunately, however, it seems that Paul reconnected with John Mark when he later requested that he be included again in Paul's ministry (2 Tim 4:11). We don't know, however, if he and Barnabas ever repaired their relationship.

Two examples in Jesus' life illustrate how others tried to triangle him in. Luke records his visit to see Martha and Mary (Lk 10:38-42). Martha was anxious to provide a great meal for Jesus. Her anxiety spilled out when she noticed Mary's apparent oblivion to her work in the kitchen. She confronted Jesus and accused him of not caring that Mary wasn't doing her part. She demanded that he correct her. But Jesus refused to be drawn into that triangle. Instead he pointed to Martha's anxiety, saying, "Martha, Martha, . . . you are worried and upset about many things" and then left her to her own choices (Lk 10:40-41).

At another time, Jesus didn't let himself get drawn into a conflict between a man and his brother's dispute about their inheritance (Lk 12:13-21). Instead he pointed to the man's greed. In both cases Jesus wanted the anxious person to deal with his or her own heart.

TIPS ON HOW TO LEARN FROM TRIANGLES AND EXPOSE UNHEALTHY ONES: THINK IN THREES

Play a grownup version of *Where's Waldo* by looking for triangles. As you deal with people, always keep in mind that most will try to handle their anxiety through triangles. Also, think beyond isolated triangles. Sometimes triangles interlock with other triangles.

For example, I once was in a triangle with two key leaders who were best friends. Let's say their names were Jimmy and George. We sometimes disagreed about ministry philosophy, but these differences were exacerbated through an interlocking triangle. One of those leaders was also a best friend with another key leader we'll call Fred, with whom I sometimes butted heads. So I was caught in two interlocking triangles with best friends. It looked like the diagram below. Because interlocking triangles often are aligned around certain issues, effecting change with these leaders became very difficult.

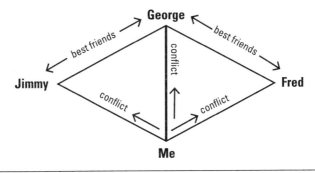

Figure 6.1.

Keep in mind that the third point of a triangle may not be a person. It may be a group, a cause or an issue. For example, let's say First Church is not meeting its budget. At a board meeting, after some research, they realize that 80 percent of the church gives very little. So a triangle forms among the pastor, the board and the "nongivers." The board feels some relief that they've found a scapegoat for the problem: the nongivers.

In a subconscious way, they've passed their burden onto the non-givers. But shifting the burden doesn't solve anything. After a while, if giving does not increase, the board shifts the burden onto the pastor for not "being visionary enough" to inspire giving from the 80 percent. Rather than blaming, a better way to deal with a giving issue would be to focus on the issue, not the people or their position in the triangle, and to create proactive solutions. So as you think in threes, remember that one point of a triangle may be an inanimate issue, yet as real as a person. A triangle would look like figure 6.2.

Often the triangles in our families of origin can give us helpful clues about how we act in our current triangles. Review the family diagram you created, and look for similar patterns in your current triangles. Think in threes there as well.

Figure 6.2.

DON'T TRY TO CHANGE THE RELATIONSHIP BETWEEN THE OTHER TWO IN YOUR TRIANGLE

If you are A, picture the other two in the triangle as B and C. Avoid the temptation to force a change in B and C, as Pastor Mark did, to no avail. I tried for years to get a leader to see another staff person differently. Even after many attempts, I never heard him say, "Charles, you're right. I don't know why after all these years I saw him like I did." In fact, the opposite occurred. The harder I tried to make the relationship get better, the worse it got. It wore me out because I was taking on their relationship tension. And for all my efforts, their relationship never improved.

I don't mean to imply that we should discourage healthy dialogue between two people in conflict. We should coach others toward healthy dialogue when appropriate. But when we try to push a relationship to get better, it seldom will. People resist such efforts.

Galatians 6:2 tells us to "carry each other's burdens" and verse 5 complements that idea with the command to "carry [your] own load." In other words, we must focus on what needs to change in us (our load) while at the same time strengthening the relationships in the triangles to which we belong. In doing so, often the relationships between the other two will improve.

MAP YOUR TRIANGLES BY TAKING A BIRD'S-EYE VIEW OF YOUR CHURCH

Take a few minutes to draw your triangles. Note the triangles where you hold the outside position. Ideally, stay in the outside position, because it is the least emotional one. Note in which direction the tension moves. Has it moved to you so that you and another person in the triangle are experiencing the most tension?

What patterns do you see in your triangles connected to church? Do you constantly have to mediate between the same two people? Have the same two people in the church constantly locked horns and drawn others into their triangle? To what degree has this historical triangle hindered ministry health? Are there structures such as a church polity, denominational issues or prior pastor issues that have formed triangles? Mapping your triangles and your church's influencers may clue you to systemic growth and health barriers. Margaret Marcuson notes, "When you learn to see triangles, you can begin to make sense of puzzling behavior in congregational life."[1]

As you map your triangles, try to map the secondary ones as well. Let's say you are in a triangle with B and C. Take a learner's stance to see if you can map out other triangles that include both B and C. Seeing them might help you depersonalize difficult relationships and think more objectively. Finally, if you find yourself in too many emotional triangles, begin to extract yourself from them, or you'll be overwhelmed.

DON'T BAIL AND DON'T DISTANCE YOURSELF FROM THOSE IN YOUR TRIANGLES

While it's important to carefully move out of some triangles, it's also important to not bail from relationships. We naturally tend to shy away from relationships in conflict. We don't want to deal with the emotionality they bring. However, distancing or bailing out often makes a relationship worse. When we keep people in the dark, which is the perception distancing often leaves, anxiety increases. As a result, people fill in the blanks and create their own skewed, negative stories about you or your ministry.

It's worth noting that sometimes we distance ourselves from others with unintended consequences, like during an extended vacation or a sabbatical. One researcher discovered that pastors who stayed in touch with their church during a sabbatical were more rested and enthusiastic about taking on their responsibilities than those who didn't.[2] I took a sabbatical many years ago in which I had little contact with the church or staff for almost two months. When I returned, I faced a hotbed of issues among the staff. In retrospect, I wish I had crafted a few all-church newsletter articles about what I was learning and doing. Short emails to the staff that I was praying for them would have been another way to keep the connection in my absence.

If you take a sabbatical, let your plan reflect your personality and what you personally need. If you are an introvert, you may need to disengage totally. If you do, create a plan that communicates your intentions before you leave. If you're an extrovert and don't mind staying in touch through pictures of what you're doing or brief updates, that's fine as well. The key is setting up expectations before you take your sabbatical.

WATCH FOR MORE INTENSE TRIANGLES IN TIMES OF CHANGE OR STRESS

When a beloved staff person leaves, when you begin a building program, when you start a significant new initiative or when stress is high in your church for whatever reason, triangles usually form with greater frequency and intensity. Be more observant during those times. Remember to take responsibility only for the relationships you are in: A to B, and A to C. Refuse responsibility for the other relationship in the triangle: B to C.

As I mentioned earlier, try to maintain the outside position in an intense triangle. If possible, stay in that least-emotional position to maintain the greatest objectivity. The key is not necessarily to get out of the triangle, but to respond to it biblically.

Focus on Issues, Not Personalities or Positions in Triangles

When we get triangled, we're tempted to take sides. The solution to the relationship problem may be obvious to us and to the offending party. However, keeping emotionally neutral can keep you from being triangled in an unhealthy way. Marcuson also offers good advice on how to respond when someone is trying to suck us into their emotional triangle and take sides. She suggests that, instead of giving a quick response to a triangling issue, you can initially say, "Let me think about that."[3]

Know the Signs When Someone's Trying to Triangle You In

Look for these signs that someone may be attempting to draw you into an unhealthy triangle.

- When someone obsesses about somebody else not doing her job, takes an unhealthy interest in the problems of others or tries to rescue another.

- When someone seems to want to get unnecessarily close to you.

- When someone focuses on you in a negative way, such as criticizing you, or in a positive way, such as flattering you. Be especially aware of flattery from someone new to the church or from someone already in the church if you are new to the church.

- When someone's reaction to you exceeds what the situation would normally dictate.

I once was in a triangle with my board and a staff member with whom I had significant conflict. I constantly felt drained from this experience. However, that staff person is now one of my best friends. How did I turn that triangle around? Over a two-year period I spent extensive time with him and listened to him with my heart. I believed that this investment would be worth my time. And it was. We grew to understand each other, and I gained a friend for life. So you can turn unhealthy triangles into good ones.

Triangles are a way of life for every pastor. I heard someone once say that we should assume that every time we speak to someone we are in a triangle. Hopefully this chapter increased your awareness that the more we know about our triangles and the better we expose the ones we are in, the better leaders we'll become and the less we'll be pulled toward people pleasing.

H. B. LONDON'S TAKE

H. B. London, president of H. B. London Ministries (hblondon.org) and pastor to pastors emeritus with Focus on the Family, writes these insights about people pleasing:

> People-pleasing is hard work. It saps our energy and often creates anxiety and anger. If you struggle with it, find a close friend who will be honest with you, who believes in you and who will speak truth to you. Before you know it, you will be pleasing to the worthy people. Also learn to be happy with yourself.

YOUR TAKE

- With what key leaders are you currently in a triangle?
- How healthy are those triangles?

7

SEARCH FOR YOUR GAPS

*Almost all problems in the spiritual life
stem from the lack of self-knowledge.*

Sт. Teresa of Avila,
The Way of Perfection

On THE ISLAND'S NORTHERN SHORE, the eerie phosphorescent screen cast a pale glow on the sides of the small trailer sitting atop Opana Peak. Lulled by the lapping waves and the tropical breeze, Joseph Lockard and George Elliott looked forward to breakfast. Having taken the night shift, their stomachs reminded them how hungry they were.

George was new on the job, and Joe, even though he was only nineteen, had been training him how to use the latest technology required for their jobs. The government had provided little formal training, so they relied mostly on on-the-job training. Their shift ended at 7:00 a.m., but since their ride to breakfast hadn't yet arrived, Joe let George practice a little longer on the device.

At 7:02 the monitor startled him when it lit up with a large, moving image, indicating an object coming toward them 136 miles due north of their position. He fixed his eyes on the image because it was completely out of the ordinary. After eighteen minutes it still appeared on the screen, which prompted George to call his supervisor about their concern. The technician who answered told him it was probably nothing.

Still concerned, he waited until he could talk to his supervisor. When he came on the line, with urgency in his voice George told him that it was the largest blip he had ever seen. The supervisor's reply? "Don't worry about it." The supervisor then explained what he believed caused the image and that he and Joe need not be alarmed.

George hung up, still not satisfied with his supervisor's analysis. Something still gnawed at him. *His explanation just doesn't add up*, he thought.

Joe and George tracked the signal until 7:39, when it disappeared off the screen. Their ride finally came, so they powered down the equipment and left, looking forward to a lazy Sunday afternoon.

Sixteen minutes later that blip exploded onto the horizon in the form of 183 fast-moving dive bombers and fighters. The rest is history.

The next day President Roosevelt described that event as America's "day of infamy." Japan had bombed Pearl Harbor, leaving unimaginable devastation: three thousand deaths, dozens of large ships destroyed and 80 percent of the American fleet of planes at Pearl Harbor smoldering in ruins.

The technology that showed the blip on the oscilloscope was the newest at the time, RADAR, and it performed as it should have. However, Army Lieutenant Kermit A. Tyler, the supervisor who told George not to worry, failed to pay attention and heed its warning message, with disastrous results. America was now at war with Japan.[1]

Had he paid attention to the blip reported by George and taken it seriously, Tyler could have alerted his superiors of danger. Although he could not have stopped the planes, with an hour's warning before they struck Pearl Harbor, the military could have been given a fighting chance to lessen the loss of life and lessen the Navy's decimation.

In a similar vein, when a pastor doesn't pay attention to the emotional blips in his own soul, he can set himself up for needless pain and diminished leadership effectiveness. Early in my ministry, I ignored the tightness in my shoulders and edge in my voice after many board meetings. Now I realize that those were emotional blips I should have paid attention to. Had I processed them, I could have been more aware of my inner world and led my board more effectively.

Most pastors today are trained to preach, counsel, lead, cast vision and develop volunteers. Unfortunately, most aren't trained to pay attention to their inner world. We seldom put self-awareness at the top of our list of crucial leadership skills. But when we don't pay attention to our subtle and not-so-subtle character gaps and emotional worlds, heartache and even disaster can overwhelm our souls and ministries, just as disaster befell Pearl Harbor because those in charge did not pay enough attention. In this chapter we look at how to become more self-aware by finding and dealing with character gaps that often fuel people pleasing.

Chapter snapshot: Search for your gaps. This chapter will draw on family systems thinking to explain how we develop pleaser gaps when we improperly manage our anxiety. It also helps you identify yourself in one or more of the five different people-pleasing patterns. You will also be able to see how your gaps compare to those of over 1,200 pastors who revealed theirs.

One of the most respected leadership voices today, Harvard professor and author Bill George, believes that self-awareness is the key to healthy leadership. He wrote his bestselling book, *True North*, around the definitive traits successful leaders embody. He wrote, "In interviewing 125 authentic leaders, we learned that the essence of leadership comes from not from having pre-defined characteristics. Rather, it comes from knowing yourself—your strengths and weaknesses—by understanding your unique life story and the challenges you have experienced."[2]

I agree with his assessment. As I've grown in my awareness of how my strengths and weaknesses rose out of my life story, I've become a more mature and healthier leader. And the more open to my emotional ruts I've become, the more the Holy Spirit has sifted and grown me. As the seventeenth-century Spanish priest Baltasar Gracián wrote, "Self-correction begins with self-knowledge."[3]

When anxiety runs high, leaders can default to unhealthy patterns, often to please others. For the short term, these patterns may help ease the tension between you and an individual, between you and your board, and tension due to other stresses. But when they become habitual patterns and long-term ruts, they can be destructive. Unless we deal with those patterns, they can dampen our long-term effectiveness as leaders. I once read about a sign on an Alaskan highway that humorously illustrates this long-term effect. It read, "Choose your rut carefully. You'll be in it for the next two hundred miles."

I earlier described phase two of my research, when more than 1,200 ministry leaders took a self-awareness inventory based on the Differentiation of Self Inventory (DSI).[4] It measured four categories of maturity that potentially indicate people pleasing. Again, in family systems terminology, the term for maturity is differentiation of self. These categories reflect what we do in relationships when anxiety gets uncomfortably high. I've put in parentheses the corresponding positive phrase, because it makes understanding the figure below easier.

- *Emotional restraint* (or in Bowen terminology, emotional reactivity) measures how well a leader thoughtfully responds to stress, problems and anxiety.

- *Convictional stance* (lack of I-position) measures how well a leader adheres to her convictions when pressured to do otherwise.

- *Connectedness in relational tension* (emotional cutoff) measures how well a leader stays relationally connected to difficult people in anxious times rather than emotionally and/or behaviorally distancing himself from them.

- *Healthy independence* (fusion) measures a leader's ability to avoid emotional overinvolvement with others, to avoid overreliance on them to confirm her personal beliefs, decisions and convictions, and to hold clearly defined convictions.

The inventory asked forty-six questions related to each of these categories on a six-point scale from "not true of me at all" to "very true of me." The lowest score for each category would be a one and the highest a six. Figure 7.1 below shows how various groups of ministry leaders self-reported.

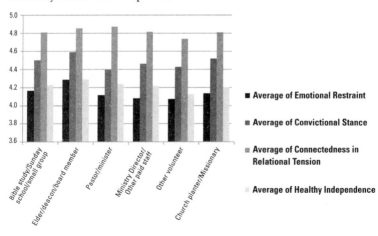

Figure 7.1.

The higher bars indicate healthier patterns, and conversely the lower bars indicate less healthy patterns. For example, in the category "Bible study/Sunday school/small group" leader, the highest bar is connectedness in relational tension (emotional cutoff). It means that this group of leaders rated themselves higher in that category than they did in the other categories.

The chart also reveals that the weakest area across all categories of ministry leaders is emotional restraint (emotional reactivity). In other words, when compared to all four domains, a ministry leader's least healthy responses to anxiety most often show up as emotional reactivity—that is, not being able to restrain emotions. Here are some fascinating findings from my surveys related to emotional control:

- Pastors with a high school education showed the same reactivity as those with a doctoral degree.

- Experienced pastors showed less reactivity than less experienced ones. Those with at least twenty years of experience showed the least reactivity. However, those with ten to twenty years showed the greatest reactivity.

- Older pastors showed less reactivity than younger ones.

- Board members indicated less reactivity than senior pastors. (Some pretty significant implications there.)

- Associate pastors showed less reactivity than senior pastors.

- Pastors in churches with an attendance of greater than one thousand evidenced less reactivity than pastors in smaller churches.

- There was no difference between the reactivity of men and women (perhaps dispelling the myth that women leaders are more emotional).

I devote all of chapter 10 to emotional reactivity. In the rest of this chapter, however, we'll look at the following four gaps, plus two other important family systems gaps the survey didn't cover: overfunctioning and underfunctioning (defined below). As you read more about these gaps, ask yourself which one is your biggest.

Loss of passion and joy

I was serving in a worship leader position. I tried to conform to what the pastor thought was important and in doing so lost a lot of passion for leading the congregation in singing. I found myself trying to please him instead of God and wasn't engaging the congregation, and my heart wasn't in the right place.

Rather than working out a vision for a ministry project that fit my strengths and giftedness, I tried to go along with someone else's half-baked plan for a ministry project. I agreed with the intended end result, but did not agree with the method or the people putting the plan together. I ended up annoyed, confused about what to do next, highly critical of the people on the project and with a sense that I was not walking in step with the Holy Spirit.

GAP 1: EMOTIONAL REACTIVITY (LOW EMOTIONAL RESTRAINT)

Description. *Emotional reactivity* shows up in us when we are under stress and either outwardly or inwardly emotionally react to others.

Metaphor. Porcupine

Characteristics. Emotional outbursts, conflict, yelling, closed body language, relational distancing, triangling, sullenness, withdrawal

Biblical character with this gap. Moses showed reactivity several times. He killed an Egyptian when he saw him beating a Hebrew (Ex 2:12). He reactively struck a rock out of frustration with the people instead of obeying God's command to speak to it (Num 20:10-11). And he threw down the first set of the Ten Commandments when he saw the people worshiping the golden calf (Ex 32:19).

Tips for growth.

- Practice mindfulness (see chapter 9) so that when emotions arise, you respond instead of reacting. This gives the Holy Spirit time to direct your response during the short window between your awareness of an impulse and your response to it.

- Memorize key Scriptures about emotional control (such as Eph 4:29; Jas 1:19).

- Practice the three tools for regulating emotions discussed in chapter 10: label your emotion, reappraise the situation and self-distance.

GAP 2: LACK OF I-POSITION (LOW CONVICTIONAL STANCE)

Description. A pastor with this gap stands on his convictions when he senses those around him would agree with him. When pressured to change his stand, he often gives in.

Metaphor. Jellyfish

Characteristics. Fear of taking an opposing position with church influences like big givers or elders, lack of backbone, blaming others, holding others responsible for her happiness or failures

Biblical character with this gap. Timothy probably faced this gap in his leadership early in his ministry life. We see this from inferences in the apostle Paul's advice to him. Paul encouraged him not to let others look down on his youth (1 Tim 4:12). He also encouraged him not to be timid (2 Tim 1:7).

Tips for growth.

- Learn to calmly state what you believe, what you see, what you think and what you will or won't do. When you state your position on an issue, do so without attempting to force change in another, reverting to another gap or getting involved in unhealthy emotional debate.

- When you take a position, take it without being abrasive or being in someone's face.

- Reflect on situations in Scripture when Jesus stood his ground (took an I-position). Luke tells the story of when Jesus traveled with Mary and Joseph to Jerusalem for the Feast of the Passover (Lk 2:41-49). Jesus got separated from them, and they didn't find him for three days. All the while he sat in the temple, amazing the Jewish leaders with his wisdom. When Mary and Joseph confronted him, he responded, "Didn't you know I had to be in my Father's house?" Jesus calmly responded to their question and stated his position.

He also took an I-position after an intense time of teaching and miracles at Capernaum, a city in Galilee. As he often did after intense ministry, he spent time with his Father in a solitary place. When the people found him, they pressed him to stay. He refused by saying, "I must preach the good news of the kingdom of God to the other towns also, because that is why I was sent" (Lk 4:43). Jesus knew his purpose given by his heavenly Father, and he stayed on course no matter the pressures to veer from it.

Gap 3: Emotional Cutoff (Low Connectedness in Relational Tension)

Description. A pastor with this gap will distance himself emotionally or physically from others when his anxiety rises.

Metaphor. A box turtle that retreats into its shell when afraid

Characteristics. Pouting, giving the silent treatment, physically distancing, switching churches often to avoid dealing with difficult relationships and emotions, rigid boundaries, ignoring others, stonewalling, passive-aggressiveness

Biblical character with this gap. The prodigal son *and* his brother. The prodigal son physically and emotionally cut himself off from his father when he left home after receiving his inheritance. After blowing his money and ending up feeding pigs, he returned home repentant. Yet when his older brother learned that their dad was throwing a welcome-home party, he emotionally cut himself off from them both by whining to his dad and then refusing to attend the party (Lk 15:11-32).

Absalom also models cutoff. After his stepbrother Amnon raped their stepsister Tamar, he emotionally cut himself off from Amnon as he plotted his murder. Two years later he murdered Amnon and then physically cut himself off from David's presence for five years (2 Sam 13–14). Ultimately his bitter heart led to his untimely death (2 Sam 18).

Tips for growth.

- Deal with emotional cutoffs in your family of origin. When you do, you will be able to deal more easily with the temptation to cut off others in your ministry.

- Know the difference between distancing and cutoff. When you distance, you create space to think about the relationship or issue so you can ultimately reconnect. Cutoff means you don't want to deal with the issue or you're avoiding it.

- Stay in relational contact with the person you're tempted to cut off.

GAP 4: FUSION (LOW HEALTHY INDEPENDENCE)

Description. A pastor with this gap gets enmeshed with others because she gets too emotionally involved with them. It's like what happens to metals when they are melted together and lose their individual distinctiveness. An Oscar Wilde quote captures the essence of fusion: "Most people are other people. Their thoughts are someone else's opinions, their lives a mimicry, their passions a quotation."[5]

Metaphor. Suckerfish (a small fish also called a remora that attaches itself to large fish through its sucker-like organ near its mouth). Another great metaphor is the Borg in *Star Trek: The Next Generation*. The Borg were creepy extraterrestrials that would assimilate humans into their hive.

Characteristics. Driven to create one big happy family, super inclusive, consensus driven, easily swayed by groupthink, herd mentality, taking responsibility for another's reactions, sense of losing self in another, seeks intense togetherness when anxiety rises, emotional temperature rises and falls based on temperature of others, greases the church's squeaky wheel

Biblical character with this gap. Aaron. Moses left him in charge when he went up on Mount Sinai to receive the Ten Commandments from God. Yet Aaron yielded to the people's herd mentality and their fear that Moses would never return because he had been gone over a month. Aaron's enmeshment with the people prompted him to make the golden calf (Ex 32:1-4).

Tips for growth.

- Seek the only legitimate relational fusion: a life deeply enmeshed in the life of Jesus. As Dr. R. Robert Creech writes, "Is it possible that an increasing 'fusion' of self in relationship with God is the only legitimate dependency?"[6]

- Spend little time trying to appease the squeaky wheels.

- Realize that when you stand alone in contrast to going along with everybody else, you will feel more anxious. It's normal. Neuroscience tells us that when we stand alone our brain's emotional circuits get activated, and we feel social pain. It's called the pain of independence.[7]

GAP 5: OVERFUNCTIONING

Description. The pastor who overfunctions is usually an overachiever who takes ownership and responsibility for the emotional well-being of others, often trying to make up for the perceived deficiency in someone else's functioning.

Metaphor. Female worker bees. They do almost every task in a beehive while the male bees look on, present only to mate with the queen bee. The female worker bees literally work themselves to death when flowers bloom; they usually die within five weeks. They die alone, away from the colony that they exhausted their lives for.

Characteristics. Very hard worker, seldom asks for help, tries too much to help, assumes increasing responsibility for others, tells others what they need to feel/think/do, does for others what they should do for themselves, often demands agreement from others, can foster learned helplessness from others, often highly approval oriented

Biblical character with this gap. Moses was probably guilty of overfunctioning when he tried to act as judge for all the disputes among the people (Ex 18). Fortunately he heeded his father-in-law Jethro's advice to delegate. Martha would be another example, evidenced in her anxiety about preparing a meal for Jesus while Mary sat at his feet (Lk 10:38-42).

Tips for growth.

- Allow others to face the consequences of their actions without acting on a desire to rescue them. Become less responsible at times.

- Practice the principle of a weekly sabbath. Take vacations. Beware of regularly working unreasonable hours. Listen to your spouse or close friend if he or she says you are working too much, stressing too often or burning the candle at both ends.

- Guard against being prideful about your productivity or your ability to accomplish more than others.

GAP 6: UNDERFUNCTIONING

Description. Pastors with a gap of underfunctioning seem always to need help but never seem to change. They don't take appropriate responsibility and often want someone else to fix them.

Metaphor. Whipped puppy

Characteristics. Highly dependent on others to know what to do next, unnecessarily asks for advice, often passive, asks others to do what she should do for herself, easily sucked into groupthink, gives in most of the time

King

Biblical character with this gap. Saul is the Bible's number-one people pleaser and underfunctioner. First Samuel 17 describes a pointed example of this gap. When Goliath taunted Saul and his men, Saul should have taken responsibility and fought him. Instead he gave that responsibility to the shepherd boy David. Saul's passivity was one of many kinks in his armor.

Tips for growth.

- Stick to the issues without resorting to blaming people for church problems.

- Ask yourself if you become passive when around high achievers or overfunctioning leaders or certain groups in your church (such as your board). If you do, exert more assertiveness and responsibility when with them.

- Delegate what should be delegated, but don't delegate responsibilities only you should own.

- Lead responsibly by staying organized, being prepared for meetings and showing up to appointments and meetings on time.

I tend to overfunction. If someone is not doing his job or is emotionally out of sync, I want to fix things. I've learned, though, that when I let someone else wrestle with his own issues and don't step in, often he works out his issues on his own. Now, if a staff member needs my help, I'll coach her by asking the right questions to steer her gently in the right direction. And I'll step in before a train wreck occurs, but I've found that when someone discovers her own solutions and faces the consequences of her own choices, what she learns will last. When I overfunction, stepping in to fix things, I rob her of an opportunity to grow.

As you read the description of each gap, did one or two resonate with you? I believe every pastor struggles with at least one. Fortunately, God promises us that by his Holy Spirit we can rely on him and he will fill those gaps. This verse encourages me when I struggle, and I hope it does you too.

His divine power has given us everything we need for life and godliness through our knowledge of him who called us by his own glory and goodness. (2 Pet 1:3)

STEVE SACCONE'S TAKE

Steve Saccone (stevesaccone.com), a leadership development expert and the author of *Protégé: Developing Your Next Generation of Leaders,* challenges us with these words:

The challenge of approval addiction originates by answering the question, "Who do you allow to control who you are?" Or ask it from another vantage point: "Who controls who you are pretending to be?" Follow the trail and how you answer those two questions will guide you towards the root of this issue in your life.

To overcome approval addiction, pastors must wrestle with the "why" questions. Why do people's perceptions and opinions matter so much to us? Why do we care more about the audio tracks of people's opinions more than God's audio track? Why do we give so much power to pleasing others and allow them to determine who we are and how we live?

YOUR TAKE

- What significant gaps do you see in your key leadership or staff?
- How could you approach them to discuss what you've learned about gaps?

8

Nitpickers and Stone Throwers

ENGAGE YOUR CRITICS

Calm, like panic, is contagious.

MARGARET MARCUSON, AUTHOR

MEN WANTED FOR HAZARDOUS JOURNEY. SMALL WAGES, BITTER COLD, LONG MONTHS OF COMPLETE DARKNESS, CONSTANT DANGER, SAFE RETURN DOUBTFUL. HONOUR AND RECOGNITION IN CASE OF SUCCESS.

Little did those accepted for this job out of the thousands who applied realize how true those words would eventually become.

Ernest Shackleton, a well-known explorer in the early 1900s, placed this ad in 1915 to recruit a team for his third attempt to cross the continent of Antarctica. In August of that year, he set sail with his recruits in the ship *Endurance*, named after his family motto: "By endurance, we conquer." Three months later they arrived at South Georgia Island in the southern Atlantic to begin their thousand-mile trek to the Antarctic Peninsula, a trip expected to take 120 days.

More than a year earlier, Vilhjalmur Stefansson had led a different expedition to explore the Arctic in their ship, the *Karluk*. Both ships endured similar fates in their respective voyages. Dennis Perkins recorded these words about Shackleton's Antarctic expedition:

> The masts toppled and the sides were stove in, as shards of ice ripped the strong timbers to shreds. Frank Wild made a last tour of the dying vessel and found two crewmembers in the forecastle, fast asleep after their exhausting labor at the bilge pumps. He said, "She's going, boys, I think it's time to get off."[1]

Both expeditions, a year apart, had been gripped in an icy vice that crushed their respective ships, forcing each party onto the ice and into horrific conditions. Yet similar circumstances, only poles apart, yielded dramatically different results. In the months following the *Karluk*'s destruction, the crew disintegrated into a conflict-laden, self-centered group, which resulted in the death of eleven of its crew.

In contrast, Shackleton's crew, although they too confronted harsh circumstances and conflict, emerged on dry land 634 days after the expedition began. Not a single man perished. Although they faced the same hellish conditions as Stefansson's men did, they experienced a different fate.

What made the difference? Shackleton's leadership presence. The ship's surgeon, Alexander Macklin, captured one of the most important leadership characteristics Shackleton embodied that contributed to the men's survival when he wrote in his diary, "Shackleton at this time showed one of his sparks of real greatness. He did not rage at all, or show outwardly the slightest sign of disappointment; he told us simply and *calmly* that we must winter in the Pack, explained its dangers and possibilities; never lost his optimism, and prepared for winter."[2]

Shackleton exemplified the quality that forms the fifth principle from the acronym PRESENT: engage your critics. In his time of crisis, he calmly connected to his men, especially the dissidents and troublemakers. It made the difference between life and death.

> **Chapter snapshot: Engage your critics.** By applying one of the key concepts in family systems, *calm presence with anxious others*, you can learn how to defuse anxiety by calmly staying connected to church critics, nitpickers and stone throwers. Neuroscience verifies the biblical principle from Proverbs ("a gentle answer turns away wrath," 15:1) that we can use to defuse other people's anxiety and moderate our people-pleasing tendencies.

Men in Shackleton's expedition noticed his calm, steady demeanor. When they were stuck on the ship, even one of his most pessimistic crewmen wrote in his journal, "He is always able to keep his troubles under and show a bold front. His unfailing cheeriness means a lot to a band of disappointed explorers like ourselves. . . . He is one of the greatest optimists living."[3]

Shackleton keenly understood the importance of setting an example for his men on how to handle conflict and stress in a crisis. As you might imagine, living under such harsh conditions could easily cause arguments and disagreements. Yet those disagreements rarely disrupted unity, because he developed an atmosphere that encouraged dissent to be brought into the open. Although he was a man of deep emotions, known even for a quick temper, he kept his composure under those conditions. He resolved problems and conflicts early, before they festered into something destructive to the crew.

Unlike Shackleton, some pastors often discourage disagreement, cut off conflict or distance themselves from critics—all motivated by a misguided desire to keep the peace and foster unity. Several years ago I hired a young staff member I'll call Sharon, who held great promise in ministry. She was smart, talented and full of energy, and although she showed some glaring weaknesses, I believed she would grow out of them. She always treated me with respect and followed my direction.

However, I began to hear rumblings that she was harsh with others on her team. At first I dismissed her critics and even refused to listen to them, mentally labeling them as gossips or divisive. I had subtly conveyed to others that I was closed to hearing about the negativity Sharon brought to the team. I finally began to listen, but not until the damage had been done. I released her, and it took a year to regain team unity.

One of Shackleton's most striking leadership qualities was his refusal to distance himself from his critics and those with whom his personality clashed. Instead he actually drew closer to those men.[4]

- His photographer, Frank Hurley, would feel slighted if the crew didn't pay attention to him and would then become difficult to work with. Instead of isolating him, Shackleton gave him a place in his tent and often conferred with him.

- His physicist, Reginald Jamer, was an introverted academic. Shackleton feared that his personality might invite ridicule that in turn could escalate into a serious issue. He made him a bunkmate as well.

- When Shackleton selected a crew to take a lifeboat to sail from Elephant Island to South Georgia Island to assemble a rescue party for the entire crew, he selected the carpenter, McNeish. He chose him not only for his skills but also because he was concerned that McNeish would create discontent with the men who remained.

- Shackleton specifically picked two other crewmen because he felt they might cause trouble in his absence. In total, more than half of those in the group he chose were potential troublemakers. The crew unquestionably followed Shackleton's leadership until

McNeish refused to go on and threatened a mutiny that would break the team's unity necessary for survival. He reasoned that the agreement that he originally made was valid only if he were on the ship. And since they had no ship, he was not obligated to continue on. Frank Worsley, the ship's captain, summoned Shackleton when McNeish made his claims. As Shackleton stood and faced the recalcitrant McNeish, McNeish lashed out. When he finished his tirade, Shackleton turned his back, walked away and left him in the snow, "giving him time to come to his senses."[5] Instead of reacting, he had taken a courageous, calm stand that allowed McNeish to settle down. The crew's unity was preserved. Eventually the crew was rescued, making this survival story one of the greatest ever.

Shackleton constantly faced four choices when confronted with dissidence, the same choices we pastors face today:

- Pander and give in to critics to restore tranquility (fusion). Often because the critics are big givers or wield relational influence in our churches, we pander to them.

- Isolate or ignore critics, troublemakers and those with whom our personalities rub, thinking that if we don't hear those voices, they will go away (cut off). In rebuilding Jerusalem's wall, Nehemiah showed the opposite tendency toward his biggest critics (see below).

- Get defensive and power up to quiet the critic.

- Show courage and stay calmly connected to the critic. I failed to do this when I refused to listen to the damage caused by Sharon, the staff person I mentioned above.

Shackleton wisely chose the fourth option.

The biblical character Nehemiah also displayed great calm and courage in the face of critics. God had given him a deep burden to rebuild Jerusalem's broken walls so he could help bring her back to spiritual prominence. As cupbearer to King Artaxerxes, he held a very significant position. He put his life on the line daily by tasting the food and wine before the king ate it. If it was poisoned, he would take the fall instead of the king.

As you might assume, the king deeply respected Nehemiah, which inclined him to respond favorably to his request to return to Jerusalem to rebuild the walls. As soon as word spread about his plan, however, critics began to raise their voices in opposition. Sanballat, Tobiah and Geshem, leaders in the area surrounding Jerusalem, began to mock, ridicule and resist in every way possible. To undermine his leadership, they publicly accused him of sedition and self-promotion. They even threatened his life.

Yet Nehemiah responded with calm and courage. He did not react nor did he relent. He trusted God, tapped into his core convictions, kept his vision focused and stood his ground. His words revealed his heart: "Should someone in my position run from danger?" (Neh 6:11 NLT).

Through Nehemiah's leadership, the wall stood complete after only fifty-two days. The critical voices then quieted: "When all our enemies heard the news and all the surrounding nations saw it, our enemies totally lost their nerve. They knew that God was behind this work" (Neh 6:16 *The Message*).

Unfortunately, influential people and even those with whom we've invested the most sometimes become our greatest critics. Such people sometimes attempt to demonize us, as did Nehemiah's critics. Edwin Friedman writes that critics can try to sabotage our calm and courageous leadership by labeling us as compulsive, foolhardy, inflexible, cold, callous or bullheaded.[6]

In one church where I served years ago, I built a great friendship with a leader I'll call Jake. He became my greatest cheerleader and often complimented me about my preaching and leading. If I could count on anybody to encourage me, I could count on Jake. Over time, however, as I stood my ground on certain issues with which we disagreed, he began to change. Compliments ceased. Frowns replaced smiles. And the emotional vibe I felt from him was more repelling than attracting—like a force field (which I'll discuss soon). Jake became my greatest critic.

During a very intense time, his rhetoric and resistance ratcheted up to an almost unbearable level. I recall one leaders' meeting when the negativity was palpable. Fortunately I kept my cool in that meeting, even though he was very harsh. As the meeting ended, still rank with negative emotions, we all stood. As I left, God prompted me to pat Jake on his shoulder as a gesture of connectedness. Had I yielded to my emotion at the moment, I certainly would not have touched him and probably would have snubbed him. Yet I believe that calm gesture, plus others the following weeks, helped us stay connected enough so that at a later lunch we were able to make things right between us.

Another leader I'll call Sally always seemed to contend with me on leadership issues. However, I would often initiate a call after a disagreement to listen further to her concerns. Later she publicly stated that our relational rubs actually helped her grow spiritually, a concept describe in Proverbs: "As iron sharpens iron, so one man sharpens another" (Prov 27:17).

Such choices never come easy, but healthy leaders choose to stay calmly connected to those they disagree with. And such leadership has more to do with our own responses than with trying to change our detractors' positions.

One pastor shared her story about Isabella, "a person who constantly criticized my pastoral work and with whom I could never do anything that would elicit a positive comment." This pastor felt like she and Isabella were in competition, as they both were pastors in the same Latin American country. Yet she didn't cut her off. She decided to spend more time with Isabella and suggested a daily walk together. They adjusted their schedules and began these thirty-minute walks.

After several weeks, she realized that Isabella just desired a bit more of the pastor's attention and wanted to learn about her previous pastoral experiences so she could grow herself. They became good friends and ministry partners, and "the Holy Spirit gave each of us insight into each other's experiences." She confidently wrote, "It was definitely worth the extra time I spent with Isabella."

It takes discernment to know how much time we should spend with our detractors. One pastor wrote, "I met too frequently and long with the critics. It took time from the positive contributors. It brought me down, sapped my energy and enthusiasm, and denied me the opportunity to spend time with the creative, encouraging movers." At some point you may realize what this pastor realized. When you do, let that be your cue to decrease your contact with detractors.

EMOTIONAL FORCE FIELDS

In Miss Pickens's third-grade class at Glen Oaks Elementary School in Fairfield, Alabama, I performed the first of many science experiments. As a full-fledged geek, I looked forward to those experiment days. One day Miss Pickens gave each of us a small, rectangular magnet about the size of a stick of gum, a sheet of white paper and a small container filled with metal filings. She told us to place the magnet on our wooden desks and then place the paper over it. Then she instructed us to slowly pour the metal filings on the paper. Magically, the metal filings clumped into semi-circular shapes at each end of the magnet. She then explained that those filings aligned themselves with the unseen magnetic force fields radiating from each end of the magnet. Thus I learned about the concept of force fields.

In the same way we all carry with us emotional force fields. You've probably met people that carry around a magnetic, attracting one. My wife does. She loves people, and people immediately sense that. They feel drawn to her because her personality and caring persona invite interaction. One the other hand, I've known people that carry around an emotional field that pushes people away. It doesn't take much interaction for me to feel uncomfortable or even repelled by such people.

Neuroscience describes a process called *theory of mind* that enables us to intuit the emotional and mental state of somebody else to some extent. When we notice someone's body language and eye movements, we subconsciously can sense his emotional state and whether he is for or against us. Although not foolproof, this ability helps us pick up on subtle cues from others and "read" their emotional force field, whether it draws us to them or pushes us away.

People pleasing led to a financial cost in one church

I changed my decision about hiring someone to build our church just to appease another. As I suspected, the work was of poor quality; we've had to pay someone else to try to fix it, and we've had problems with the building ever since. My appeasement caused the church to pay double.

Appeasement made one pastor feel disempowered

In the first year of my first pastorate (after having been in ministry ten years), I raised a topic with my leadership team that was evidently divisive. I wanted to keep talking about it as a team to work through the issues, but because a couple of parties strongly suggested it was not a topic that should be raised, I was afraid to do so. Since I process thoughts best in conversation, and since the leadership team as a whole didn't agree about discussing it, the subject sat. Then I proposed we do some preaching/teaching on the topic, but the team was hesitant. Now I feel disempowered from free inquiry and exploration of the topic in any congregational setting.

An episode in the book of Ruth illustrates the idea of force fields. When the women in Bethlehem first saw Naomi years after she had left with her husband, they were shocked at what they sensed in her. Her name, which meant "pleasant," no longer described her countenance. Instead, her losses in the previous decade had led left their mark, and the women immediately sensed it. No longer "pleasant," she asked them to call her Mara, which means "bitterness" (Ruth 1:19-20).

In a similar fashion, I could often sense Jake's mood simply by looking at him. He would sometimes come into a meeting with an emotional field that screamed, "I'm in a bad mood, and I'm going to resist everything you say." His entire persona telegraphed his adversarial mood. In contrast, I recall another leader in our church that always carried an emotional field that said, "Charles, I am for you and with you. I support you."

When we step into another's emotional field, it does affect us. We often function in unhealthy ways in response to these fields. When I sensed the adversarial leader's mood, I would often subconsciously tense up. My anxiety level would rise, and I would put myself on guard for fear of being hurt in some way. As a result, I could not think as clearly and would easily become defensive.

On the other hand, when I sensed another leader's affirmative mood, I felt safe. I could be myself, listen and be fully present for her. This experience parallels how the poles of magnets either repel or attract each other. Difficult church conditions often give rise to repelling emotional fields that can cause conflict, personality clashes and distance.

When we find ourselves in these adversarial fields, we must draw deeply from our spiritual resources, as Nehemiah did. Instead of disconnecting, powering up or reacting, we must stay calmly connected to that person. Our responses significantly affect the emotional fields of others in a positive or a negative way. When we keep our cool in the face of conflict, we think more clearly and can actually moderate the person's or the group's overall anxiety.

Consider Canada geese, for example. When I lived in Chicago,

I'd often jog in the fall near a field packed with resting geese. When I ran near them, inevitably one would crane its neck, look at me and stand up, which caused the rest of the flock to do the same in a ripple effect. The one goose's "anxiety" fed the others'. But after I ran by (unless for fun I ran at them), that initial goose would lower its neck and sit down, which cued the rest of the flock to follow. Its anxiety, or lack of it, affected the entire flock.

That's how it works in churches. It travels from person to person in groups. If a pastor brings his anxiety into a staff meeting (or a church service), it likely causes everybody else's anxiety to rise as well. Likewise, if he relates to others with calm instead of anxiousness, they mirror his calmness. As Margaret Marcuson writes, "When a leader is clear, calm, and confident, people find their own confidence increased, and they are more likely to follow."[7]

Calmly connecting does not mean we never get emotional or show passion. Nor does it imply we should become best friends with our critics. Roberta Gilbert explains it this way:

> If the leader can make a more frequent contact with difficult people (notwithstanding the fact that we all want to distance from them) they will often settle down. These contacts don't have to be large amounts of time, they simply need to take place. And, sometimes, they don't need to be about issues. Contact simply needs to be made.[8]

I recall a particularly emotional interaction in a meeting with Jake. The entire emotional field that night rose to ten plus because I reacted to him. I enabled his immaturity by my immature reaction. On the other hand, in another meeting when Jake acted in an adversarial way, I kept my cool and maintained my poise and calm. I listened and was able to keep the entire meeting much calmer by my example. I didn't allow his emotionality (or mine) to hijack the meeting.

It's not that I didn't feel emotions inside. I did, but I chose not to act on them in an unhealthy way. I practiced a simple mental technique we'll unpack in chapter 10: *label your emotion; don't suppress it.* Marcuson writes, "If we consider our perspective as calmly as possible, that calm communicates itself to others. Anxiety is contagious, but so are thoughtfulness and calm."[9]

If I could "do over" my relationships with my critics and detractors, I would spend more time with them, but not as a people pleaser. One of my ruts is to cut off from others when I feel uncomfortable or threatened. Had I calmly connected with those people more frequently, I could have avoided lots of tension, crises and unnecessary anxiety. Travis Bradberry and Jean Greaves write, "The weaker the connection you have with someone, the harder it is to get your point across. . . . The difference between an interaction and a relationship is a matter of frequency. It's a product of the quality, depth and time you spend interacting with another person."[10]

Friedman reinforces this thought with these words:

> If a leader will take primary responsibility for his or her own position as "head" and work to define his or her own goals and self, while staying in touch with the rest of the organism, there is a more than reasonable chance that the body will follow. There may be initial resistance but, if the leader can stay in touch with the resisters, the body will usually go along.[11]

TIPS FOR ENGAGING YOUR CRITICS AND MINIMIZING PEOPLE PLEASING

Take the initiative. Make a list of critics in your ministry that you currently avoid and with whom you need to (re)connect. Pray that they will respond to your initiatives to reach out. Ask the Lord to give you the courage to act. And determine the best way to reach each individual. Should you schedule a breakfast or lunch with him? If you do, be sure to communicate that you don't have an agenda but that you simply want to connect. Or should you seek her out after a church service to chat?

Perhaps you should perform a simple act of kindness. I once dealt with a leader who would often casting a wary eye toward me. It seemed that I could never meet his expectations. He rarely affirmed me, and although he was not necessarily an open critic, his emotional field around me was seldom an attracting one.

I knew his wife enjoyed gardening, and loved unique gardening tools. I saw an interesting hand tool in a flight magazine on a plane trip, so I ordered it for her. A few days after she got it, this leader gave me one of the few compliments I ever got from him; he thanked me for my thoughtfulness toward his wife and seemed truly appreciative. That small act of kindness helped keep me connected to this critic.

As you increase the frequency of contact with your critics, you will build trust. Someone once said, "Trust is a peculiar resource; it is built rather than depleted by use."

One final thought: some critics are so caustic that you need to keep your distance. Remember, you don't need to maintain contact with every critic. Use your judgment.

Leverage the power of story. Learn to share your story regularly with others. Let your critics know who you are and what makes you tick. That doesn't mean you must share every intimate detail. Rather, open your heart to let others in. Be vulnerable to them.

At the same time, learn your critic's stories as well. In a non-intrusive way, express curiosity about his life and his story without overdoing it with questions. God may give you a broader perspective and insight to what fuels his criticism.

Put yourself in your critic's shoes. Instead of mentally tagging her with a negative description, reframe your self-talk. Ask yourself, "I wonder why Jill acts likes she does. I wonder what she brings from her past that could be fueling her criticism." Adopt a learning mindset rather than a judging one.

One way to share your story is through passion. I'm an introvert, and although I have good people skills, I'm not a party person. If given a choice, I'd rather read, be in a quiet place, connect one on one and stay out of the limelight. When on stage, though, I communicate passion. But I've realized that in day-to-day encounters, my introverted personality can sometimes convey to others that I lack passion, especially to extroverted leaders.

When trying to connect with extroverted leaders, sometimes I've tried to force passion, which unfortunately can come across as emotional reactivity. I'm now learning to communicate more of my heart and passion through story, while staying true to how God created me. I now share more of my life when I preach and when I lead meetings. So, if you're an introvert like me, you'll probably have to work harder to communicate passion than if you're an extrovert.

Become more self-aware. When someone criticizes you, learn to become more aware of both your internal and your external responses. Although we should never let others crush us with unhealthy criticism, when we listen with an open heart to constructive feedback, the critic's anxiety often lessens. The Bible says, "You can trust a friend who corrects you" (Prov 27:6 CEV).

Our body language, facial expressions and eye contact can make things either worse or better. Neuroscientists have discovered something called *mirror neurons*. This part of our brain subconsciously mimics what we see in others. If your critic sees a relaxed, caring persona or a smile, this subconsciously encourages him to mirror you. The writer of Proverbs understood this principle long before neuroscientists did, wisely noting, "A gentle answer turns away wrath, but a harsh word stirs up anger" (Prov 15:1)

To strengthen self-awareness, try to listen to others without mentally framing your response. As Shackleton did when McNeish attempted mutiny and spewed his anger, remain calm and wisely refuse to give an immediate response. Catch yourself if you begin to form a response in your mind while your critic is still talking.

Ask clarifying questions so you can see your critic's viewpoint. Toward the end of such a conversation, ask the person, "Is there anything else?" Then thank him for giving you feedback, even though you may disagree. If the conversation warrants a later response, tell him you'd like to think about what he said and get back with him later. And don't forget to do so.

Keep your critics in the loop. Don't keep significant critics in the dark. Where appropriate, include them when you make decisions. "Explain your decisions. Don't just make them."[12] Explain the *why* behind your decisions, and acknowledge the impact they may have on others. In doing do, you are subtly engaging critics in the decision process.

At the same time, acknowledge your critic's emotions when you make a decision about which he may have disagreed. If you make a decision contrary to his wishes and you sense he's angry with you because he avoids you at church or through some other behavior, a simple call to check in could make huge deposits into that relationship. A conversation might go like this: "Jim, I sense your concern about the decision I made. I respect you and don't want our relationship to suffer because of it. Would you like to talk about it sometime?"

One caveat though. Don't allow inappropriate behavior. Staying connected does not preclude biblical confrontation if your critic becomes divisive or begins to hinder the ministry. Remember, staying connected involves both calm and courage.

Provide a face-saving "out" if necessary. If possible, avoid putting your critic into a situation where he loses face in front of others. I once came across so strong to a critic in a meeting that the only way he could save face was to power up and react, which he did. From that point on, our emotionality hijacked our meeting. Scipio, a Roman general, understood this principle. He "advised giving opponents a 'Golden Bridge,' an avenue of retreat, arguing that an enemy with no way out will fight with unprecedented ferocity."[13]

Don't catastrophize. Guard against making catastrophes out of conflicts, blowing situations out of proportion. The human brain is hard-wired to magnify negativity. Neuroscientists use the term *affective forecasting* to describe the mental process of predicting how we think we will feel about a future event. Simply put, we aren't very good at accurately predicting our emotions in the future. We tend to over-predict the intensity and duration of our future emotional reaction. With criticism we tend to overstate how we will feel when criticized and understate our ability to cope with the effects of it on us personally. We also tend to predict that others will feel as anxious in the future about the issue as we currently feel. When this happens, we engage the fight-or-flight part of our brain, which makes us more likely to react to our critics. So remember, the intensity and impact of criticism is often much less than we predict.

That's why Jesus admonishes us in Matthew 6 not to worry. He also said to not "worry in advance" (Lk 21:14 NLT); it only makes things worse. Satan will capitalize on our tendency to catastrophize and tempt us to blow criticism (or expected criticism) out of proportion. So when you know a critic is coming your way, remind yourself that it probably won't be as bad as you expect and that you will probably be able to respond better than you think you can.

When tempted to catastrophize, view your critics in a different light. Friedman told a story about a famous pastor who began to think of his detractors as his "loyal opposition." "By conveying that he thought their attacks on him were a sign of *duty* rather than *subversion*, he eliminated almost completely from his own behavior the anxious feedback that is necessary to sustain chronic conditions."[14]

Stay playful. Keep a sense of humor and defuse tension with a good dose of playfulness. Sometimes our intense seriousness can create an atmosphere so heavy that it sabotages our meetings and interactions with others. Don't shy away from challenging others with courageous leadership, yet stay loose by interjecting fun and humor into tense situations. Humor can help us connect to our critics by softening an otherwise heavy atmosphere. Use discernment, though, to know when to use humor and when to avoid it. Sometimes we can wrongly use humor to divert discussion from difficult issues.

A Final Word

We can't force or contrive a calm presence with others in the heat of the moment. In less than a quarter of a second, our bodies begin a neurological process that can cause an emotion that we can't consciously stop. We can't stop the feeling, but by God's grace we can control its expression. Paul reminds us, "You, however, are controlled not by the sinful nature but by the Spirit, if the Spirit of God lives in you" (Rom 8:9).

Although we can't contrive a calm presence, we can offer the gift of peace to our churches, our team and our leaders if we stay closely connected to the God of peace himself. Knowing who you are and whose you are will provide the basis for such leadership strength. In chapter 5 we looked at the concept of revisiting and anchoring your values. With such anchors, you can calmly connect to those who oppose you.

While writing this chapter I read a blog entry that beautifully illustrates where calm presence comes from. This author used Murray Bowen's phrase for calm presence: *non-anxious presence.*

Julian of Norwich, though not officially ordained in the church, filled the priestly role when in her *Revelations of Divine Love*, she wrote, "All shall be well, and all shall be well, and all manner of things shall be well."

Julian was no pie-in-the-sky starry-eyed idealist. Julian of Norwich was a child when the bubonic plague first reached England. Within her lifetime nearly half the population of England died from the plague. Julian had seen suffering, pain, sorrow, and human tragedy beyond imagining. Yet, Julian could peer into the face of this desperate affliction and declare, "All shall be well, and all shall be well, and all manner of things shall be well."

This is the leadership of the "non-anxious presence." Julian was able to offer this leadership, not because she believed everything in life always ran smoothly, but because she had found within herself a place of peace and steadiness. She had made the journey, in a time of great suffering, to her own non-anxious place.[15]

LANCE WITT'S TAKE

Lance Witt, former executive pastor of Saddleback Church and author of *Replenish* and founder of Replenish Ministries (replenish .net) offers these wise words to help us avoid and conquer people pleasing:

> Pay attention to what's going on inside you. Ask good questions about your motives . . . questions like, "Why do I care so much what they think?" Or "What's behind my inability to say no?" Identifying and naming the brokenness is a great first step in letting the Holy Spirit break our bondage to people's approval.

YOUR TAKE

- Does the suggestion "Stay close to your critics" bother you?
- Why or why not?

Self-Care

*NURTURE YOUR SOUL
THROUGH MINDFULNESS*

*I just keep concentrating on the present moment.
I forget the past and preserve myself from
worries about the future. When people
become despondent and fainthearted
it is because they are thinking
about the past and the future.*

THERESE OF LISIEUX

As Nicholas began his trip to purchase supplies, he knew the pain would get worse with each step, as it had for years. As a young soldier, his near-fatal war injury had severely damaged his sciatic nerve, leaving him almost crippled in one leg. With every labored step, intense pain would shoot down his hip and into his leg.

When he finally arrived at the port to purchase supplies, the only way he could move around the boat was to roll clumsily over the wine casks. Yet this hindrance didn't seem to dampen his peace and tranquility. Even on his deathbed decades later, his friends marveled at the joy they saw in his face and in his speech. During those last hours, he even asked to be rolled over to his painful side to "bear just a little for the love of God."[1]

Nicholas was born in France around 1611. A fire during the Thirty Years War, the war where he received his near-fatal injury, destroyed his birth records. As a result, we know little about his early years or his exact birth date. We do know from his writings that he humorously described himself as a "footman who was clumsy and broke everything."[2]

In the winter of 1629, he noticed a leafless tree. He began to think about the coming spring when budding leaves and new fruit would refresh the tree. This image reminded him of God's power, providence and love and ultimately led to his conversion.

In his midlife, Nicholas entered a newly established monastery in Paris. Although he disliked his first assignment, working in the kitchen, he developed a remarkable perspective. Even though standing for hours compounded his pain, he never complained. He believed that he should give God his unbroken attention, not just during formal times of prayer, but also during menial tasks like washing dishes or cleaning the kitchen. Even through the clatter of dishes and the pressing demands from the one hundred members in the monastery, he described his experience with God in the kitchen "as great tranquility as if I were upon my knees at the blessed supper."[3]

His simple message was this: practice the presence of God moment by moment. Over three hundred years later, a compilation of his short letters and written conversations remains and describes how Nicholas developed this unbroken intimacy with God. The short booklet, *The Practice of the Presence of God*, has encouraged untold numbers of believers to nurture their walk with Jesus by paying attention to him moment by moment. Today we remember this amazing man not by this birth name, Nicholas Lorraine, but by the name given him when he entered the monastery, Brother Lawrence.

Brother Lawrence learned how to make himself fully present for God every moment, how to walk continually in his presence even in the midst of chronic pain and mundane circumstances. He left an example of how we can know God's peace and presence regardless of our circumstances by being fully present in his presence. He modeled for us the sixth principle PRESENT leaders embrace: nurture your soul through practicing Christ-centered mindfulness.

Chapter snapshot: Nurture your soul through mindfulness.
Soul care is an often overlooked and underpracticed discipline for a busy pastor. With sermons to preach, leaders to lead and people to shepherd, it's easy to neglect our soul. But Scripture commands us to tend to our soul, and Jesus modeled it through time with his Father. This chapter looks deeper into a pastor's soul care. When we tend to our soul through biblical mediation and mindfulness, we can actually change our brain, which helps us both moderate people pleasing and manage our emotions better. Thus we become better leaders. In this chapter we'll delve into mindfulness as a biblical practice that can help us nurture our souls.

Nurturing your soul, at first glance, may seem intuitive and a bit elementary. Most of us need little convincing that we should prioritize our spiritual growth. In this chapter, however, I focus on a different kind of spiritual discipline not as commonly practiced as ones like prayer and fasting. I certainly agree that the basic spiritual disciplines are integral to spiritual growth, and I regularly use them. But Brother Lawrence practiced something not usually included in the standard list of disciplines: mindfulness.

Mindfulness, as the name implies, involves engaging our minds to enlarge and deepen our souls. This practice helps us more consistently live in the present moment instead of in the disappointments of the past or the uncertainties of the future.

Before I continue, it's important to draw distinctions between Christian mindfulness and Buddhist mindfulness. Buddhist mindfulness strives for an empty mind to reach a so-called nirvana, a state where all desire is vanquished. Mindfulness for a Christian, however, leads us to declutter our minds so that we fill them with God's truth and a correct view of realty. Its goal is not to create an empty mind but a mind renewed by Christ. Also, our view of God stands in stark contrast to a Buddhist's view. For a Buddhist, God is unknowable. But the goal for Christian mindfulness is to use this tool to help us know God more deeply, as Brother Lawrence did. So Christian mindfulness stands in stark contrast to how Buddhists would define mindfulness.

Mindfulness addresses our mind's tendency to be flighty and prone to distraction. Think of your devotional times with the Lord. I imagine you, like me, sometimes struggle to stay focused. Intrusive thoughts pop into our minds when we try to concentrate on the Lord and his Word. Giving another person our full attention while listening to him is hard to do as well.

Recall a leadership meeting when you felt verbally affronted by a leader. You probably found it difficult to tune in to that person because your mind subconsciously began to frame your response even while she was talking. As consistent as Brother Lawrence appeared to be in being present moment by moment, he understood the difficulty of living in the present, because our minds are so easily distracted.

> You are not the only one who is troubled with wandering
> thoughts. Our mind is extremely roving. But the will is mis-

tress of all our faculties. She must recall our stray thoughts and carry them to God as their final end. If the mind is not sufficiently controlled and disciplined at our first engaging in devotion, it contracts certain bad habits of wandering and dissipation. . . . One way to re-collect the mind easily in the time of prayer, and preserve it more in tranquility, is not to let it wander too far at other times. Keep your mind strictly in the presence of God.[4]

In my favorite Brother Lawrence quote, he sums up the goal of Christian mindfulness: "Above all, get in the habit of often thinking of God, and forget Him the least you can."[5]

People pleasing affected the excellence in one church

As a music minister, I once tried to appease people by allowing musicians to be on the team who weren't gifted, for the sake of inclusiveness. My appeasement caused an overall decline in our band's quality and ultimately I had to reverse my policy.

Appeasement can lead to a loss of respect and credibility

I dropped a program that I felt we really should be doing, because of some who voiced their disapproval. Now I feel my decision cost me, diminished my integrity and hindered others wanting to follow my leadership. I was frightened to confront a woman and her husband who had offended several people in my congregation, so I remained silent. I lost credibility with those who were grieved by this couple and felt the truth of the old adage that "silence is not always golden; it is sometimes yellow!"

MINDFULNESS: WHAT IS IT?

The Western world tends to be "on" 24-7. Our smartphones vibrate when a text message arrives. Our computers alert us to new emails. And the Internet keeps us up to date with world news around the clock. We tend to pay partial attention, continuously, to make sure we're not missing anything. Once we were enjoined to manage our time. Now, with multiple information sources, we must manage our attention as well. Linda Stone, an author and speaker, coined the term *constant partial attention*. It's a mental trap we easily fall into when we constantly scan our surroundings to look for the best opportunities to spend our time on.

Pastors easily fall prey to this with the demands ministry places on us. On Sunday mornings, as we chat with a visitor, we're tempted to look beyond her to see who else we need to talk to. During our devotional time, thoughts about the day's tasks often intrude. After a Sunday service, as we shake hands with people, this nagging thought can sometimes surface: *I wonder if they liked my message today?* When driving, our phone keeps us always available. Our attempts to multitask hinder us from being truly present in the moment for others or for God. Our brain too easily flits from one thought or distraction to the next as a butterfly flits from one flower to the next.

Mindfulness is a spiritual tool that combats continuous partial attention by helping us live in and appreciate the present moment. It also helps us moderate worry, people pleasing, fear and anxiety. It's a whole-life experience we shouldn't reserve just for a quiet time. It's a discipline that should permeate our preaching, counseling, family time, leading, relationships with others and even re-laxation time. By living in the moment, we are most able to be fully present to God and fully present to others, as we saw in Brother Lawrence's life. Being fully present means disengaging from auto-matic thoughts, feelings, memories and reactions. It's a heightened and healthy sense of self-awareness in real-time, as we accept what we see and experience in the moment.

BENEFITS OF MINDFULNESS

Being mindful isn't hard; remembering to do so is. When we do remember to practice mindfulness, it benefits us in many ways.

- We can catch and silence people-pleasing brain chatter, that inner dialogue we're often unaware of. Someone once said that you can't control the train of thoughts coming your way, but you can decide whether or not you want to get on the train.

- Mindfulness helps us position our hearts to experience every moment as an opportunity to see God in it, as Brother Lawrence did.

- It helps put space between an impulse and a behavior. Being aware of our thoughts can help us stop and think before reacting unconsciously on an emotional impulse. Mindfulness helps us be *in* the moment rather than doing something in response *to* the moment. In less than a quarter of a second, our body responds to external stimuli. In the next quarter of a second, we become aware of our body responding. In the next fraction of a second, we choose how we'll respond to that impulse. Mindfulness puts space between the impulse and the action. That extra fraction of a second allows us to be more thoughtful about how we will respond, thus giving us more choices instead of mindlessly reacting.

- Focus and you'll be a better listener. Instead of partially listening to someone else while framing your response while he's still speaking, you'll be able to hear him fully first.

- You will be able to sense the promptings of the Holy Spirit more readily. Remember, God spoke to Elijah not through thunder and lighting, but through a gentle whisper (1 Kings 19:11-12).

- It helps us avoid unhealthy preoccupation with ourselves and become more focused on God and others.

- It helps us view our emotions and thoughts as transitory events instead of ascribing those thoughts and emotions as necessarily true of us; it keeps us from overly identifying with them, as they may or may not reflect reality. Mindfulness helps us not only notice an emotion or thought, but also realize that such a thought or emotion is not "us." For example, let's say you hear that a pastor friend of yours had twice the attendance last Sunday at his church than your church did. You may feel an immediate impulse of jealousy. Mindfulness helps you step back and look at that feeling as simply a feeling and quite possibly one with no sinful motive behind it. It can help you see these thoughts and emotions as passing events. Or it may lead you to realize that you've got some spiritual work to do on comparing yourself with others. So mindfulness helps us *describe* emotions and thoughts rather than instantly *ascribe* meaning or value to them. It helps us see emotions and thoughts as subjective, in contrast to something necessarily valid, and transitory, in contrast to something permanent.

- The medical world has discovered that mindfulness is good for our physical health in several ways: it strengthens our immune system, it slows the aging process, and it helps us better manage chronic pain.[6] It's also been shown to decrease anxiety and depression.[7]

Biblical Support for Mindfulness

The word *mindfulness* as applied to people doesn't appear in Scripture. However, the Bible does tell us that God himself is mindful of us (Ps 8:4; Heb 2:6). He pays careful attention to us because he cares for us and loves us. Even though the word itself does not appear, several Scriptures reinforce the concept.

- In Psalm 37:7 and Psalm 46:10, the psalmist tells us to be still. Mindfulness helps us to still our hearts and bodies mentally and physically before the Lord.

- Multiple times in the Psalms we see King David meditating on God's words and works. Meditating on his Word is a powerful way believers can be fully present with him. The ancient church fathers often practiced meditation when they separated themselves from worldly distractions.

- In Luke 10:38-42, Jesus commends Mary for sitting at his feet while at the same time he mildly rebukes Martha for letting busyness rob her of what was most important. Mary gave Jesus her full presence; Martha gave Jesus her partial presence. She was there in body, but her soul was preoccupied with cooking dinner and with her anger at Mary for not helping. Mary was mindful of Jesus; Martha was not. Her mind flitted from cooking to Mary to Jesus to her anger and then again to cooking to Mary to Jesus to her anger. I image this cycle kept repeating itself.

- In Psalm 131:2, King David describes himself stilling and quieting his soul like a weaned child with his mother. As a weaned child finds contentment from simply being with her mother, so does a believer find contentment when she's mindful of the Lord.

- Isaiah 26:3 says that if we steadfastly keep our minds on the Lord, he will give us his peace. The word *steadfast* means "to lean on." Mindfulness helps us lean into and on the Lord more consistently.

- In Matthew 6:25-30, Jesus commands us not to worry about tomorrow. He preached this passage outside as part of what we call the Sermon on the Mount. I imagine as he taught about worry, he pointed to the birds that flew by and to flowers in the ground nearby as object lessons. He drew the attention of those listening to the here and now, the present moment, to teach these important spiritual truths.

- In 1 Kings 19, God told Elijah to stand on the mountain, for he was about to appear. God spoke not in the whirlwind or the earthquake or the fire. Rather, he spoke in a gentler whisper. Elijah had to pay careful attention in the moment to hear God in that whisper.

Mindfulness will bring richness to your devotional times with God. But as Brother Lawrence modeled for us, it's not something reserved only for our private times with God. Mindfulness is a way of living that can nurture your soul around the clock. Whether in the bustle of a crowd at church, an intense staff meeting or a heated conversation with a critic, it can help you stay focused on the Lord and draw from his strength.

THE BRAIN AND MINDFULNESS

David Rock, one of today's leading voices in applying neuroscience to life and leadership, explains how pervasive mindfulness has become in our world.

> Today, some people refer to the experience of observing yourself as self-awareness or mindfulness. Sometimes it is called metacognition, which means "thinking about your thinking." Or meta-awareness, which means "awareness of your awareness." Whatever it's called, this phenomenon is a central thread in much of the world's literature, appearing as a core idea in philosophy, psychology, ethics, leadership, management, education, learning, training, parenting, dieting, sports, and self-improvement. It's hard to read anything about human experience without someone saying that "knowing yourself" is the first step toward any kind of change.[8]

I would add spiritual formation and Christian leadership to his list. Unfortunately the church is often slow to adopt new ideas from the business world or science. But since all truth is God's truth, it behooves Christian leaders to learn more about how our brain influences our leadership—and in our case, how it influences our drive to please. The more we understand about our brain and its effects on mindfulness, the better leaders we'll become.

Recent neuroscience findings have helped us more clearly understand mindfulness. God gave all of us the ability to create mental representations of our outside world, called maps (also called modes, circuits or networks). Whatever we pay attention to over time creates these maps. If you're a pastor, crafting a sermon would be a map for you, whereas framing a house might be a carpenter's map.

Neuroscientists have discovered that our brains carry two different sets of maps, or circuits, through which we intersect with the world.[9] One is the default map; the other is the direct map. We use the default mode when not much else is happening. This network, like its name suggests, is active most of the time and takes little effort to operate. Our thinking subconsciously defaults to our default maps. This network gets activated when we daydream, let our mind wander and think about ourselves.

The brain has the ability to store a massive amount of information about us and about others we interact with. When the default network is activated, like a giant tapestry, it weaves together vast amounts of information about the future and the past. It draws from memories about others and about ourselves stored in our brains. The direct network, however, relates to real-time, direct experience. When this network is active, different brain regions engage, including the areas that detect bodily sensations and those that direct where we place our attention.

These two networks operate in inverse fashion. That is, when one is active, the other is not. Say, for example, on your way to church on Sunday you're deep in thought about your sermon (you're using your default network). You find that road construction has changed your normal driving route. Instead of paying attention to the signs (your direct network), you stay immersed in your sermon (your default network). As a result, you miss a turn and get lost on the way to church. When you finally drive into the parking lot, you're late and you've become anxious. Had you paid attention to what was happening in the moment (direct mode), you would have seen the signs and made it to church on time without getting anxious.

Mindfulness is a learned skill that can help us more easily switch from one mode or network to the next, because we must operate out of each mode at the appropriate times. Consider this example about switching: A few years ago I faced a serious issue with a key leader in a leaders' meeting. Things got heated in that meeting, and it ended with no resolution. A few days later, my emotions were still raw. While trimming some bushes in my backyard, I became oblivious to the shears whacking a bush. Why? My mind had wandered back to that leadership meeting, and I had begun an internal argument with that leader. It felt as if I were actually back in that leadership conference room arguing with him, emotions and all. My mind was stuck in my default network in a bad way.

Fortunately, something caused me to pause and yell out loud, "Stop!" I stepped back and became aware of my mentally contrived argument. I then was able to view the situation more objectively, realizing that my internal dialogue was only getting me angrier and not providing a solution. When I yelled, "Stop," I took a third-person perspective of myself, as if I were looking at myself through the viewfinder of a camera. When I took that third-person perspective, my anxiety began to diminish, I began to think more clearly, and I was able to stop the contrived mental argument. At that time I had just started to practice mindfulness by thinking about what I was thinking about and had experienced a few successes. Since then I've become more consistent in applying mindfulness.

Switching from the default to the direct mode is not that difficult. It's remembering to do so that challenges us. If you want to begin trying mindfulness, pay close attention to chapter 11. In that chapter I lay out a simple, seven-day mindfulness training process that begins with your daily devotional time. If you follow that plan and start building mindfulness into your life, it will help you not only catch and counter people-pleasing thoughts, but also stop other unhealthy thinking patterns. Of course, the best way to experience mindfulness is to practice it.

Tips About Mindfulness to Consider

Mindfulness is essentially the discipline of training your attention on the present. You might want to keep in mind these four concepts as you try the seven-day mindfulness plan in chapter 11:

- *Intention.* Mindfulness is not a technique to distract yourself, but a way to intentionally tune in to the present moment. It requires that we remember to live intentionally in and experience the present moment.

- *Presence.* Mindfulness is paying attention to what *is* at the moment rather than focusing on we want *different* in that moment. It means not allowing our thinking to ruminate over past hurts, disappointments or broken dreams or to worry about the uncertainty of the future.

- *Nonjudgmental.* Mindfulness is being open and receptive to the moment without judging our thoughts and emotions. It's *noticing* rather than *ascribing value to* our thoughts and emotions. It's suspending quick judgment to allow time for measured reflection.

- *Beginner's mind.* Mindfulness is approaching our thoughts and emotions as a child might approach something new, with curiosity. It's a way to learn from the moment while minimizing the influence from our preconceived notions and biases.

As you experiment with mindfulness and learn to make it a regular part of your soul care, I believe you will discover it to be a rich source of growth. Although leaders who aren't prone to being contemplative may find it more difficult, even they can find strength by closing their door during a busy afternoon and stilling their soul for a few minutes. Making mindfulness a way of life can enrich your walk with God, help you catch and banish people-pleasing thoughts and give you God's peace in turbulent times.

RUSTY HAYES'S TAKE

Rusty Hayes is the senior pastor of the First Evangelical Free Church in Rockford, Illinois (firstfreerockford.org), one of the largest Evangelical Free churches in the United States. He offers these wise words to help us avoid people pleasing:

> I've heard it said that the number one fear in America is public speaking. I can relate. Public speaking means people are watching, evaluating, making judgments . . . about me. Yikes! The problem is that pastoring involves a lot of public speaking, public meetings, public eating, and public everything! Being a pastor is fraught with the temptation to be what I think people want me to be. To overcome, I've had to turn repeatedly to God for my affirmation while insisting to myself that I will be authentic. Being real and having a real, sustaining relationship with God have been my antidotes to the consuming need for popularity. Only then does the public become subject to the higher purposes of Christ in my heart and I don't worry so much about things like how you are currently evaluating this quote.

YOUR TAKE

- How would you rate the priority you currently give to soul care?
- To what degree do you believe mindfulness could help you care for your soul better?

Are Your Reactions Showing?

TAME YOUR REACTIVITY

> *To the extent that leaders . . . can maintain a*
> *non-anxious presence in a highly energized*
> *anxiety field, they can have the same*
> *effects on that field that transformers*
> *have in an electrical circuit.*
>
> EDWIN FRIEDMAN

FOR MONTHS THE ISSUE HAD SIMMERED. Hopeful that it had died down, he excitedly planned the next deacon's meeting to share his new vision for the church. Pastor John never expected the meeting to go so horribly wrong and to result in "The Email" the next day.

John had come to Central Baptist nine years earlier after the former pastor had abruptly resigned. During John's leadership, the church had grown, although not dramatically, as the area's population was static and several new churches had started nearby.

But good things had happened, and the unity in the church was as high as it have been in years—except at the deacon-board level. The church had begun forty years prior in an elementary school in a state in the western United States (this is a true story with details altered). The leadership structure was a board of four plus the pastor. All four board members were fast friends, two of them since high school. The other two met weekly in an accountability group. They often interacted socially with each other, but seldom with the pastor.

During a board meeting a few months prior to The Email, one of the deacons, Henry, smiled, looked at John and said, "Pastor John, you're a great guy and I have nothing personal against you, but I don't believe you have what it takes to take the church to the next level."

John sat stunned. Questions swirled in his mind. Why didn't he talk to me personally before springing this on me? What about me does he think I lack to lead the church effectively? Was this a roundabout way to ask for my resignation? He didn't know what to say, except "Oh really?" The rest of the meeting was a blur. Toward the meeting's end, one of the other board members, William, said, "John, go and pray about this, and let us know if you believe God wants you to continue as our pastor." As they adjourned, John thought, What kind of suggestion was that?

As you might expect, the next several weeks were difficult. Yet John had no sense that his time at Central was over. At the next monthly meeting, he told the board that he felt that God still wanted him to lead the church. The board then voted to affirm his leadership role, and John thought the issue was dead.

About halfway through the following meeting, Henry again brought up the issue. "John," he said, "I just don't believe you have what it takes to lead our church to the next level."

John quipped, "I thought you had affirmed my leadership?"

"We did, but I can't deny my feelings."

A sinking feeling filled John's stomach. In the weeks that followed, he soldiered on, but his thoughts often drifted to what the deacons really felt about him.

At the next month's meeting, Henry again said, "John, I don't believe you have what it takes to lead our church." By this time John was sick of hearing it, but he kept his cool during that meeting. The next week he asked a wise pastor friend how he should respond should the issue come up again. His friend encouraged him to tell Henry that the issue had been decided and that he should not bring it up again.

As expected, at the next meeting Henry said the same thing. In a firm tone, John took his friend's advice and asked him not to bring it up again, because the issue had been settled. When he said this, Henry exploded in rage and began to rant, which pushed John's emotions even higher. John yelled, "So, do you want me to resign?"

Henry retorted, "Yes, I do!"

As John's defensiveness peaked, he looked at the other members and yelled, "Do you the rest of you also want me to resign?"

William quickly said yes, and the other two said little. After Henry ranted for a few more minutes, he stood up, sternly stated, "I quit!" and stormed out. Things quieted down for the remaining ten minutes before the meeting adjourned. As it did, William asked John to think about things and get back with him.

John slept very little that night. He had read about these kinds of board meetings, but he never thought he'd find himself in one. The next morning he emailed one of the board members and asked that a mediator be brought in to help with the conflict. In two hours the member emailed back with, "We do not think we need a mediator. The board made a decision last night, and next week we will send you a letter about it."

A decision? John thought. Puzzled, he emailed him back and asked that the letter be emailed to him. Ten minutes later he received The Email. He had been summarily fired.

In the weeks that followed, after much counseling, John eventually saw God's hand in his dismissal, although he wished the board had handled it differently by including a neutral third party. He realized that even if he had not blown up in that meeting, he would not have been able to stay much longer at Central. More importantly, he realized that his defensiveness and reactivity had exacerbated the conflict that night and had accelerated the deacons' decision to dismiss him.

Although you may have never faced such an emotion-laden board meeting, we've all probably reacted to someone in our church or family in a way that worsened a situation. In John's case, his multiyear attempt to gain the deacons' approval had failed. Ultimately his frustration at this failure surfaced in his defensiveness in that meeting. In this chapter, I explain how we can stay cool under pressure and hopefully avoid disastrous elevations in emotionality that can hinder kingdom progress.

> **Chapter snapshot: Tame your reactivity.** This chapter focuses on emotional reactivity. Through insights from neuroscience, I show several practical ways leaders can stay cool under pressure with their families, boards, fellow staff and others in the church. Hopefully, by heeding these insights, pastors can avoid disastrous elevations in emotionality that can hurt their effectiveness. I also explain the eight Fs of people pleasing related to reactivity.

A leader's mood profoundly influences those around him as people tend to reflect their leader's tone, whether it's good or bad. A strong PRESENT leader, in contrast to a pleaser leader, can defuse emotionality by his calm presence (recall chapter 8's subtitle: "Engage Your Critics"). In John's case, his defensiveness heightened the deacon's emotionality. Had he known some insights about how his brain worked, perhaps the process could have been more redemptive. Let's look at some insights.

....

My dad was an electrical engineer and filled his shop in our basement with the most amazing gizmos. Transistors, capacitors, transformers, electrical tools and every conceivable gadget lined the shelves and entertained me for hours. My favorite gadget was a neon sign transformer. A transformer is a device that either steps up or steps down current. The metal green box in a yard down your street or the cylindrical container on a telephone pole near your house is a transformer that steps down high-voltage power to 220 volts that comes into your house.

With my dad's neon sign transformer, I made what is called a Jacob's ladder. I attached two three-foot wires to the leads on each side, and bent the wires into a V. When I plugged it in, a multi-thousand volt spark started at the bottom of the V and arced to the top. In this case, the transformer stepped up the household current to over two thousand volts. My Jacob's ladder created lots of really cool sparks that appealed to my geekish interests. And I got shocked by it only once.

A leader is like a transformer. By her responses, she can either defuse an emotional setting like a heated board meeting or can act like a step-up transformer by reacting and increasing anxiety, thus causing lots of not-so-cool sparks, as did Pastor John. Through a calm presence with emotional people, a leader can act like an emotional step-down transformer, decreasing the group's anxiety by letting it pass through her without getting zapped.

Jesus experienced the full range of human emotions. He wept when he heard that Lazarus had died. He became angry at the temple moneychangers. He felt a heavy heart in the garden of Gethsemane. Yet his behavior reflected anything but anxious reactivity.

Jesus' response to his enemies throughout his trial and crucifixion, as 1 Peter 2:23 illustrates, continues to amaze me: "When they hurled their insults at him, he did not retaliate; when he suffered, he made no threats. Instead, he entrusted himself to him who judges justly." Every time I recall this verse, I stand in awe. Although he possessed God's power to destroy his detractors, he didn't. Rather, he leaned into his heavenly Father to respond appropriately to hardship. Likewise, as we lean into our heavenly Father, he gives us what we need to say no to reactivity.

The Bible tells us that the Lord has given us everything we need to live a godly life. Second Peter 1:3 is so powerful as it encourages us with these words: "His divine power has given us everything we need for life and godliness through our knowledge of him who called us by his own glory and goodness." God has crafted our bodies and brains, our souls and minds, and our regenerated hearts with the capability to cool our emotions in the midst of emotionality. Acting calmly when tempted to do otherwise glorifies him.

Sometimes we characterize emotionality simply as defensiveness, as we saw in Pastor John's reactivity. But chronic anxiety that fuels emotionality shows up in eight ways that I call "the eight Fs of chronic anxiety." It manifests itself differently in different people. As you read the list below, consider which F tempts you the most.

- *Fight*: emotionally reacting and becoming defensive (how we usually describe emotionality)

- *Flee*: emotionally or physically cutting off from others in anxious situations

- *Freeze*: not knowing what to do, thus not taking a position; offering no opinion and/or staying neutral when you should take a position

- *Fuse*: losing your identity by glomming on to others' wants and desires, compromising convictions, seeking unity at all costs and/or trying to force everybody to be one big, happy family

- *Fixate*: easily getting triangled into unhealthy relationships and conflict

- *Fix*: overperforming to fix somebody else's problems or doing for others what they should do for themselves

- *Flounder*: becoming passive, underperforming, or giving up

- *Feed/fornicate/finances:* inappropriately yielding to base impulses by turning to food, illicit sex/pornography or inappropriate use of money

Let's look at insights about the brain that can help us fight these eight Fs of chronic anxiety.

Trying to make others happy pushed this pastor to explode

A popular musician was hurting the church by his gossip and refusal to update his musical selections. I tried to keep everyone happy but ended up so stressed that I exploded at him and said things I was sorry for.

INSIGHTS ABOUT THE BRAIN

Certain brain processes can increase the likelihood that we yield to one of the eight Fs. In their book *Switch,* Chip and Dan Heath borrow a helpful analogy from Jonathan Haidt's book *The Happiness Hypothesis* to describe two fundamental brain processes at work in decision making. I borrow that same analogy to explain our inbred tendency toward emotionality. A rider perched atop an elephant represents our emotional side (the elephant) and our thinking side (the rider). Although the rider holds the reins and seems to be in control, the elephant often does what it wants when it wants.

Likewise, it seems that emotions regularly take the upper hand over clear biblical thinking, often reflected in one of the eight Fs. We don't want to react to an elder who disagrees with us nor do we want to yell at our son who talks back to us. We don't want to click to a webpage and look at inappropriate pictures of women. Neither do we want to give a key leader the cold shoulder because he criticizes us. Unfortunately, we often do the opposite of what we want. Our emotional side often pushes our thinking side to the passenger's seat and takes control in the driver's seat. Paul describes this spiritual battle: "I do not understand what I do. For what I want to do I do not do, but what I hate I do" (Rom 7:15). When this happens, what's going on inside our brain?

The limbic system, a collection of structures deep inside our brain, houses our emotional side. Within those structures lie twin grape-sized clusters of cells called amygdalae. When we feel threatened by something or someone, our amygdala (I'll use the singular going forward), which is primed to look for the negative, instinctually kick-starts several physiological processes to put us in a survival, fight-or-flight mode. God gave us this ability to help us survive in the face of danger. When the amygdala activates, it begins several cascading bodily events that send hormones into our bloodstream and neurotransmitters into our nervous system to heighten our ability to survive. The limbic system is great at reacting to situations but poor at thinking about them.

For example, if I'm driving in my car and a truck pulls out in front of me, I don't want to think about putting on the brakes. I want my foot to slam the brake pedal automatically to prevent a wreck. When this process occurs, respiration, heart rate, sweating and other physiological functions all increase. Our digestion slows down so that energy can be diverted to our muscles if we need to fight off something that threatens us (like a potential wreck).

So our bodies instinctively respond when we feel threatened—and not just when we feel physically threatened. The amygdala starts the same process when we feel social threat or threat to our personhood, as in Pastor John's case.

The amygdala acts like a smoke alarm, but in our bodies. Smoke alarms are always on. Just as a smoke alarm sounds an alarm when it detects smoke, so the amygdala sends an alarm to the brain stem and other parts of the brain to begin automatic processes. In the case of impending physical harm, the motor centers of the brain take over, and we run, scream, strike back, get goose bumps, hold our breath or freeze. When our self-esteem, status or leadership feels threatened, our body experiences similar responses.

Let's play out a hypothetical issue with your board. It's the first Tuesday of the month, when your board regularly meets. A small group in your church has been grumbling about your leadership. After you open the meeting with prayer, one of the most vocal elders immediately speaks up and says something like this: "We've been talking to a lot of people about your leadership. They don't like how you are leading the church. We need to talk about this."

What happens in your brain? The exact same process that you experience when a truck pulls out in front of you. The elephant (limbic system) detects a threat, this time to your leadership or perhaps even to your job and your ability to provide for your family. Your brain immediately sends signals that begin the process I just described. Your anxiety level jumps. You feel a need to protect and defend yourself.

Unless you yield your responses to the Holy Spirit and use some of the ideas I suggest below, your elephant will take over and wreak havoc. And when anxiety overwhelms clear thinking, it can affect your leadership in these ways:

- Impulse can overwhelm intentions.
- Instinct can sweep aside imagination.
- Reflexive behavior can close off reflective thought (you lose perspective).
- Defensive postures can block out defined positions.
- Emotional reactivity can limit clearly determined direction.[1]

However, we don't have to become hostage to the elephant. As the rider, empowered by the Holy Spirit, we can maintain composure when tempted to yield to one of the eight Fs. So, what brain processes are active when the rider is in control?

The rider is roughly equivalent to the executive center of our brain, the prefrontal cortex (PFC), the area directly behind our forehead. This part of our brain is one of the distinctive features that separate us from the rest of God's animal creation.

The PFC allows us to do these things:

- Experience hope. Planning takes place here, and planning can make us hopeful about the future. Hope gives us purpose for living.

- Relate to others beyond self-interest. We experience compassion and empathy here, among other brain locations.

- Reflect, look inward, stand back and be conscious about what we're thinking and doing.

- Imagine and be creative.

- Judge, solve problems, think critically and fashion values and principles by which to live.

- Regulate our emotions and exercise self-control, thus controlling the elephant.

When Jesus taught, he challenged his listeners to think critically and to reflect on God and his truth. He often asked reflective questions. He calmly stated his positions. He spoke about the future. He taught us to serve others, thereby challenging our self-centered survival motives. Jesus expects us to engage the thinking part of our brains. He certainly speaks to our emotional lives, but as I once heard a speaker say, "Jesus wants us to walk by faith and not by feel."

TIPS FOR STAYING COOL UNDER PRESSURE

When we feel tempted to react, practically speaking we need space between our initial perception of a situation and our response to it, so that we can respond thoughtfully. As the apostle James wrote,

"Take note of this: Everyone should be quick to listen, slow to speak and slow to become angry, for man's anger does not bring about the righteous life that God desires" (Jas 1:19-20). Creating this space allows time for us to yield to the Holy Spirit so that our values determine our responses, not the elephant. It's creating a tiny window of opportunity between impulse and action for God to work. It buys time for us to think first before we act.

So, what can we do when anxiety rises and we feel tempted to react? First, let's look at an insight about a part of the PFC that serves as an emotional brake. It's called the ventral lateral pre-frontal cortex (VLPFC) and is located slightly below and behind our temples. Neuroscientists have discovered that it quiets emotions that are being processed up from the limbic system deeper in our brains.[2] That is, emotional arousal ascends from the lower parts of our brain and emotional control descends from the upper parts of our brain (PFC). When we practice mindfulness as a way of life (chapter 9), we're able to more consistently catch ourselves in that tiny window of time (less than half a second) between impulse/perception and action/response.

These three practical ideas, gleaned from neuroscience, help us create that space so the Holy Spirit can recruit our emotional brake to control the elephant:

1. *Label your emotion.* Often when we feel negative emotions, we try to suppress them, especially when we are around others. We push them down, grin and bear it, or put on a happy face so that others don't see them. It's not that we're necessarily trying to make the emotions go away; we just want to suppress their appearance.

Neuroscientists have discovered that it takes a great amount of energy to do this. Often a rebound effect occurs. The harder we try to push down a negative emotion, the more we reinforce it. When we attempt to suppress such an emotion, it actually increases activity in our emotional brain circuits. It also depletes the mental resources we need to think clearly and thus respond appropriately.

It inhibits memory by dampening attention to the current conversation that may have stirred our emotions. As a result, because we're paying more attention to our emotional response (and trying to stuff it), we often miss key information outside us.

The better solution is to label your unpleasant emotion. Simply acknowledge that you feel it. If you're in a heated staff meeting and you feel your emotions rise, mentally pray, *Lord, right now I'm feeling pretty angry. I acknowledge this and ask you to help calm my emotions.* Or you might break for a few minutes and verbally tell yourself the same thing outside the boardroom. For lingering emotions, journaling is a practical way to label and process emotions.

It seems counterintuitive, but neuroscientists have discovered that labeling actually does quiet the amygdala and activates your emotional brake (VLPFC).[3] Children taught to label their emotions have been shown to perform better in school. I believe Peter's admonition "Cast all your anxiety on him because he cares for you" describes this technique in action (1 Pet 5:7). Casting our anxiety implies we must name our anxiety. The psalmist also illustrates this concept when he often verbalizes his painful emotions.

2. Reappraise the situation. Reappraisal is simply thinking about a situation differently. It's choosing to see the glass half full instead of half empty. As Barney Fife would say, reappraisal helps us "nip it [an emotion] in the bud." Paul reminds us to focus our thoughts on the positive: "Finally, brothers, whatever is true, whatever is noble, whatever is right, whatever is pure, whatever is lovely, whatever is admirable—if anything is excellent or praiseworthy— think about such things" (Phil 4:8).

Perhaps an example will help. I'm a fairly good listener. When someone talks to me, I look at her and try to give her my full attention. Likewise, when I'm listening to someone preach or teach, I do the same thing. I don't let my eyes wander, even if I'm bored. I look straight at the speaker and try to affirm her with my body language and nods. So I expect others to do the same when I speak; attentive listeners give me energy when I teach.

So it bugs me if someone constantly looks down at the floor or to the side. I once had a doctor in my church who seldom looked at me when I taught. I had to fight an internal dialogue something like, *I must be boring this morning. He just doesn't like me. He doesn't like my preaching.* This self-talk interfered with my concentration. Over the years, however, I've realized that some people are auditory learners. They're listening even when they appear not to be, like when they stare at the floor.

Reappraisal has helped me reframe how I view who I perceive to be a nonlistener. Instead of fighting negative self-talk, I tell myself, *He must be an auditory learner, so he's averting his eyes to listen to me. The Holy Spirit must really be working on his heart.* When I do this, I free up more of my thinking brain. This allows me to focus more intently on my message and to stay sensitive to the Holy Spirit, thus helping me teach more effectively. Granted, I may be fooling myself. He may indeed be bored with my message. Even so, reappraisal definitely helps me focus better.

Essentially, reappraisal helps us think about distressing situations in different ways to minimize distress. It's the ability to see an emotional situation differently in order to change its emotional significance. Putting others in your shoes can help you reappraise— that is, you can tell yourself that most people would feel what you feel in similar circumstances. At a brain level, this provides a sense of control and certainty, and the brain loves certainty. It also helps increase the neurotransmitter dopamine, which engages the rider and quiets the elephant.[4]

3. Self-distance. I've found this tool extremely effective in calming my emotions and reducing my reactivity. Self-distancing is taking the third person's perspective of a situation instead of viewing the situation as the first person, immersed in it. It's becoming a fly on the wall and observing yourself in the situation to gain insight by putting some emotional distance between it and you. It's like looking at yourself and the situation through the viewfinder of a camera.

Several years ago we sold our house. If you've ever sold one, you know the stress it creates. The buyers wanted a few plumbing issues fixed, so we called a plumber. The morning he was to arrive, I left to exercise, while my wife was to meet him. When I finished, I called her for a status check. She said, "Oh, he said the problem is so simple that you could fix it."

My elephant began to stomp around, and I asked, "So, he didn't fix it?"

"No."

"Did he charge us anything?"

"Yes, a hundred dollars."

Before I continue, it's important to understand that I was exhausted at this point in our house-selling process. And since I'm no handyman, I was willing to pay a plumber to fix the problem. But when she said he left it for me to fix and then charged us, my elephant went berserk. I felt defensive and came across very defensive in my call to her.

I sat in my car and fumed. Then I recalled what I had recently learned about self-distancing. I then imagined myself stepping out of my Nissan truck and looking at me through the viewfinder of a camera. When I did, I laughed and thought, *How silly to react that way.* Immediately I felt my emotional level drop (the amygdala quieted), and I thought more clearly (I engaged my PFC). I called Sherryl, apologized for my reaction and calmly asked her to call him to come back and fix the problem, which he finally did. Had I caught myself between impulse and action, I could have avoided my defensiveness.

Neuroscientists have found that self-distancing helps us in many ways.

- It decreases our feelings of that emotion.

- It provides better resolution to the issue.
- The emotional issue becomes less central in our lives.
- We become better equipped to deal with similar issues in the future.
- We experience less intrusive thinking (that is, when thoughts about the issue keep popping into our minds).[5]

So if John were to relive that board meeting, how could he apply these emotion regulation ideas? First, as he began to feel his emotions rise, he could internally label them by silently praying, "Lord, this situation is getting emotional. Right now I'm feeling anger rise up. Please help me control it by your Spirit."

If the emotions continued to escalate, he could suggest to the board that they break for five minutes. He could take that time to be alone to reappraise. He could audibly tell himself, "Well, as difficult as this is, it's not the end of the world. God's grace is sufficient. I know he will help me make it through this."

Finally, when the meeting reconvenes, if emotions continue to run high, he could assume the "fly on the wall perspective" and observe himself. Additionally, John could meet with the deacons individually a few days later, after emotions calm, and share what he's learned about how the brain works. In that meeting he also could suggest that the deacons craft a policy that could guide them when emotions get out of hand and good thinking takes a back seat.

Although our limbic system (the elephant) is a force to be reckoned with, God gave us the Holy Spirit and our PFC (the rider) so that we can keep unhealthy emotionality in check and avoid the eight Fs of chronic anxiety. When we practice these techniques, they will become more innate and help us become more consistent PRESENT leaders.

I offer one final observation. These simple techniques have been proven to moderate negative emotions and defensive behavior. But we often default to rumination, constantly revisiting a negative situation and the accompanying negative emotions. We mull over it, chew on it and wallow in the emotions. Obviously that's an unhealthy response, and we shouldn't ruminate.

But sometimes a ministry issue can become so painful that no matter what we do, we can't seem to control the elephant. In that case we need an objective voice, such as that of a coach, a counselor or a wise friend. When the techniques I've suggested above don't work, please seek help. God often uses godly men and women to help us regain perspective and put the rider back in control.

DR. ELMER TOWNS'S TAKE

Dr. Elmer Towns (elmertowns.com), cofounder of Liberty University, makes these observations about people pleasing:

> It is a continual threat to pastors (pleasing people rather than pleasing the Lord). Pastors must focus their attention on what John the Baptist said, "He must increase, and I must decrease" (John 3:30 NKJV).

YOUR TAKE

- Are you more of an imploder or an exploder?

- Think of the last time you reacted emotionally. What triggered it? Was that trigger a common trigger that you need to pay more attention to?

The Placebo Pastor

*Am I now trying to win the
approval of men, or of God?
Or am I trying to please men?
If I were still trying to please men,
I would not be a servant of Christ.*

THE APOSTLE PAUL (GAL 1:10)

THIS CHAPTER'S TITLE may seem inappropriate as a title for a final chapter. In today's vernacular, the word *placebo* refers to sugar pills given to patients for various illnesses. Although the pill has no medicinal value, the patient does not know that. The origin of the word, however, provides a memorable word picture for people pleasing.[1]

In the thirteenth and fourteenth centuries, the Catholic Church began practicing a ritual called the Vespers of the Office of the Dead. As part of the service, the priest leads the people in prayers for the dead. In the first chant, the congregation responds to the priest by chanting the Latin translation of Psalm 116:9: "I will please the Lord in the land of the living" (the correct translation is actually "I will walk before the Lord in the land of the living"). The Latin is *Placebo Domino in regione vivorum.* You'll notice that *placebo* is the first word in the chant. It means "to please."

In France in the Middle Ages it was a custom for the mourning family to provide food to attenders immediately after such a service. Often people unrelated to the family would attend, claim to be a relative and fake their grief so they could receive food. Over time these fakes were collectively labeled "placebo singers." They were also called "choral placaters," because they used their chant only to flatter in order to get something. They personified all things useless because they simulated grief. It wasn't genuine.

Placebo continued to convey a negative meaning and appeared as a character name in Chaucer's tales *Placebo*, about a flattering yes-man. The word began to make its way into medicine, and *Hooper's Medical Dictionary* of 1811 first defined a *placebo* as "any medicine adapted more to please than benefit the patient."

So the word *placebo* is a good mental hook for remembering the essence of people pleasing. Pleaser leaders, like placebos, may please others, but they seldom truly benefit them. Yet the chanters' original intent was to verbalize their desire to please the Lord. As Blaise Pascal wrote, "There is a God-shaped vacuum in the heart of every man which cannot be filled by any created thing, but only by God, the Creator, made known through Jesus." We fill that vacuum only when we love and please the Lord.

Yet people pleasing points to a legitimate human desire. I want people in my church to like me. I want my board and my staff to like me. But I can't let my identity rest in whether they do or don't. I can't demand that others like me. I can't allow my desire to be liked to cause me to compromise who I am or whose I am. I can't allow my life to be driven by a fear of criticism, rejection or not getting liked. I can't allow my sense of well-being to be determined by whether or not someone likes me. A true sense of well-being lies in delicately balancing loving God, loving others *and* loving ourselves.

This is easier said than done. Tim Keller helps us see how we can do it. In his short but profound book *The Freedom of Self-Forgetfulness*, he describes the apostle Paul's key to personal freedom, taken from 1 Corinthians 3:21–4:1. He says that our culture today attributes many problems to low self-esteem. So if that's the source, it seems logical that we should boost our self-esteem. Keller also points to our drive to gain approval from others, the impetus behind people pleasing. However, he notes that Paul points to a different solution to our drive for self-esteem and approval.

> Paul is saying to the Corinthians that he does not care what they think about him. He does not care what anybody thinks about him. In fact, his identity owes nothing to what people say. It is as if he is saying, "I don't care what you think. I don't care what anybody thinks." Paul's self-worth, his self-regard, his identity is not tied in any way to their verdict and their evaluation of him.[2]

For Paul, boosting our self-esteem by getting another's approval doesn't work. Rather, healthy self-esteem comes from a gospel-centered life. Keller writes, "True gospel-humility means I stop connecting every experience, every conversation, with myself. In fact, I stop thinking about myself. The freedom of self-forgetfulness. The blessed rest that only self-forgetfulness brings."[3]

As you attempt to apply these concepts, put on your lab coat, so to speak, and prepare to face resistance. When you apply the PRESENT principles, you may be shocked at how some respond to you. Some may tell you that you are wrong and that you need to change back—and if you don't change, you will face regrettable consequences. If that happens, don't be surprised by it and don't ignore it or avoid it. With God's strength and wisdom, apply the PRESENT principles anyway. These "change back" responses come with the territory as your grow and develop. Remember the concept of homeostasis (equilibrium) in an emotional system? When you begin to change, you will stir things up.

When that happens, draw on his grace. Be willing to position yourself to face challenges and hear criticism. Graciously clarify your convictions over and over. And above all, look to the Lord. He promises us everything we need to honor him and to serve others well. Remember, Jesus refused to be anxious (Mt 6:25-34). He didn't let others dictate his decisions (for example, he resisted Satan's temptation in the wilderness, Mt 4:1-11). He pointed to our need to work on *us* rather than to try to change others (that is, get the log out of your own eye first, Mt 7:1-5). And he told us to conform to him rather than to the demands of others (that is, love him more than others, Mt 10:37-39). Only through Jesus can we stand against the temptation to people please.

As you face the pressure to change back, remember these wise words Paul gave Timothy, his young protégé: "But you, keep your head in all situations, endure hardship, do the work of an evangelist, discharge all the duties of your ministry" (2 Tim 4:5).

In *Overcoming the Dark Side of Leadership*, Gary McIntosh and Samuel Rima use a compost pile to illustrate the work of the Holy Spirit. Just as time turns garbage into something useful, so the Holy Spirit takes our broken places, failures and people-pleasing traits to transform them into traits more like his. They quote a section from an insightful article written by Judy Cannato:

> The image of the compost pile articulates . . . that deeper part of the self that understands what cannot be expressed in words. What the process of composting tells me is that

there are parts of my personality that are not usable in their present form, but are nevertheless indispensable, because they provide the raw materials for personal growth. Composting also teaches me that I am responsible for participating in the process of identifying what is in need of transformation, by putting my refuse in a designated place, and then waiting as transformation occurs. Composting asks me to trust that I will eventually bear witness to what only God can do.[4]

As I've grown wiser as I've aged, God has taken my people-pleasing tendencies and thrown them into my compost pile. As life experiences have turned over that spiritual compost, I've seen God use the PRESENT principles to transform me. I've been forced to look at my past and learn from it. And he has helped me crystalize the core values that now guide my life and leadership.

My triangles have served as tools in God's hand so that I've experienced what the writer of Proverbs says: "As iron sharpens iron, so one man sharpens another" (Prov 27:17). My gaps, often glaring, have driven me to his throne of grace. I continue to see him narrow them, albeit slowly at times. My critics have stung and often rejected me. Yet God has used them to give me a tiny taste of Jesus' sufferings.

As I have sought more to *be* for God rather than *do* for God, he has enlarged my soul to love him and others more deeply. I still have a long way to go, but his grace is enabling me to *react* less often and *respond* more often. He continues to fashion me to become more of a PRESENT leader, rather than a pleaser leader.

He can do the same in you.

I leave you with the verse I quoted in the introductory chapter. It captures God's desire that we seek to please our Lord and Savior, Jesus Christ, above all else. May God richly bless your journey of life and leadership.

For my part, I am going to boast about nothing but the Cross of our Master, Jesus Christ. Because of that Cross, I have been crucified in relation to the world, set free from the stifling atmosphere of pleasing others and fitting into the little patterns that they dictate. (Gal 6:14 *The Message*)

The Leader's Toolbox

I hope the principles I've shared will have a long-term positive effect on you and your leadership as you learn to resist people pleasing and become a stronger PRESENT leader. However, simply reading a book seldom produces lasting change. True spiritual transformation occurs when we create new habits by engraining new thinking patterns into our minds and hearts. Learning best occurs when we apply what we are taught.

In this section I've included two helpful tools: a seven-day devotional plan that can help you experience mindfulness and an eight-week development plan you can use to deepen the PRESENT principles in yourself or your team. I believe that twenty to thirty minutes of weekly application will pay great dividends for you and your leadership teams.

THE SEVEN-DAY PERSONAL
DEVELOPMENT PLAN

Be happy in the moment, that's enough.
Each moment is all we need, not more.

MOTHER TERESA

Chapter snapshot. This chapter shows how to develop a spiritual practice called BEETS that can help you change pleaser habits through biblical mindfulness. The short daily readings summarize a key insight, give Scriptures and quotes for reflection and suggest a template to help drive home one concept from the BEETS process. Eighty-seven pastors participated in a research study using this concept, and their feedback indicated that this practice helped.

Although anecdotally we're told it takes twenty-one days to create a habit, it probably takes longer. With the Holy Spirit's help, we can change our thinking and thus impact our leadership. Earlier I mentioned Hebb's law, the holy grail of learning discovered by Dr. Donald O. Hebb, a Canadian psychologist prominent in the seventies and eighties. Hebb's law essentially states that neurons (brain cells) that fire together wire together. In other words, repetition can change our brain's wiring. We don't have to stay stuck in unhealthy or sinful thinking patterns. We can develop new ways of thinking and create new habits.

I liken this concept to how a footpath in a forest grows. If a path gets little foot traffic, it stays small. But the more often people walk on it, the larger, more visible and more permanent it becomes. Likewise, the more we repeat biblical thoughts and behaviors, the more they get ingrained into our hearts and become habits. The apostle Paul referred to this dynamic when he wrote, "Do not conform any longer to the pattern of this world, but be transformed by the renewing of your mind" (Rom 12:2). In this chapter I've included a devotional process that can help you become a more consistent PRESENT leader through creating a daily habit of Christian mindfulness. I believe that habitual Christian mindfulness, as discussed chapter 9, is perhaps the single greatest key to changing people-pleasing thinking and behavior.

Due to the limitations of a book, I've only included a seven-day plan. Changing mental habits takes much longer. Ideally you'd practice this process over months to make it habitual. However, seven days should acquaint you with it enough that you can build it into your devotional routine until it becomes second nature.

The third phase of the research involved eighty-seven pastors who tested the seven-day process I outline below. They took the DSI before and after so that I could see if it made a difference. The DSI measures four areas of leadership maturity related to people pleasing: emotional restraint, convictional stance, connectedness in relational tension and healthy independence. The research results showed a statistically measurable increase in emotional restraint. Although the changes weren't huge, I was encouraged that positive movement occurred after only seven days. I hope you will experience similar growth.

DAY 1

Set aside fifteen minutes each day for the next seven days when you can be alone in a quiet place to complete these devotional exercises. Then follow the simple instructions I provide. Since this is your first day, it may take a bit longer than fifteen minutes. And you may find that taking more than fifteen minutes each day will benefit you the most. It's fine to take longer.

Orientation to the seven-day process. Each day you will begin your devotional by following a process called BEETS, which I explained below. The acronym represents steps you'll complete during the first part of your devotional. Another acronym, RIPE, stands for four additional steps that you will follow as you interact with each day's Scripture. After you finish the seven devotions, consider applying both the BEETS and the RIPE process to your own devotions thereafter.

Although completing these steps may seem mechanical at first, as you practice them, they won't seem as rote. Please go through each step in the sequence I suggest. I also encourage you to write down your thoughts and impressions daily in a journal.

Let's begin with BEETS. Today I will briefly explain what each letter of BEETS stands for. You'll want to first read through the explanation I've given for each letter below. Then go back to B and take one to two minutes on it. Then work your way through the next three letters of BEETS, completing the respective exercises that I explain. You'll spend one to two minutes on each of the first four letters. Finally, you'll spend the last ten minutes on S.

B (body awareness)

As you pay attention to your body at this very moment, what is it telling you?

Get comfortable in a chair or couch where you won't be interrupted. Close your eyes and ask the Lord to help you focus. Starting at your feet, mentally envision a scanner slowly moving up through your body: your feet, your legs, your torso, your fingers, your arms, your shoulders, your neck and your head. Try to become aware of any body sensations, such as tenseness, tightness, soreness, a clenched jaw, an aching joint, a tight muscle and so on. As you detect any of these, try to relax yourself and get into the most comfortable position.

Reflect a few moments on this verse, and tell the Lord that you want to submit your body to him today as his temple: "Do you not know that your body is a temple of the Holy Spirit, who is in you, whom you have received from God?" (1 Cor 6:19).

Take about a minute or so on this exercise.

E (environment awareness)

As you pay attention to your immediate environment at this very moment, what are your five senses telling you?

With your eyes still closed, listen to the sounds around you. Don't just listen to the ones that immediately come to your awareness, but listen more deeply. Do you hear a clock on the wall? If you are outside, do you hear birds chirping or the rustling of leaves? Do you hear people talking? Pay attention to what your other senses are telling you. Do you feel wind on your skin? What do you smell? If you open your eyes, what are they drawn to? Focus on what your senses are telling you at this moment.

Now reflect a few moments on this verse, and thank him for his creation and the five senses he's given to your body: "I praise you because I am fearfully and wonderfully made; your works are wonderful, I know that full well" (Ps 139:14).

Take about a minute or so on this exercise.

E (emotions awareness)

As you pay attention to your emotions at this very moment, what are they telling you?

Pause and become aware of the emotions you are currently feeling. Are you angry, anxious, fearful, joyful, pensive, reflective, sad, happy, depressed? Whatever negative emotions you feel, acknowledge them. Don't stuff them, and don't ruminate on them. Simply name them what they are. You are not judging them, just acknowledging them. Seek only to describe your emotions rather than ascribe or attach meaning to them.

Reflect a few moments on this passage, and tell God that you want to submit your emotional responses to the Spirit's control today: "But the fruit of the Spirit is love, joy, peace, patience, kindness, goodness, faithfulness, gentleness and self-control. Against such things there is no law" (Gal 5:22-23).

Take about a minute or so on this exercise.

T (thoughts awareness)

As you pay attention to your thoughts at this very moment, what are you thinking about?

Think about what you are thinking about. Imagine seeing yourself through the viewfinder of a camera. What are your thoughts right now? Are they about something that happened yesterday, last night or last week? Are they about what you are planning to do today, tonight or tomorrow? Are they about an issue in your church, family or personal life? Are your thoughts negative or positive? As you did with your emotions, simply acknowledge your thoughts; don't judge them. Describe them rather than ascribe or attach meaning to them. Reflect on this verse a few moments, and tell the Lord that you want to submit your thought life to him today: "We take captive every thought to make it obedient to Christ" (2 Cor 10:5).

Take about a minute or so on this exercise.

S (soul awareness)

As you pay attention to your soul at this very moment, what is God impressing on you?

Read this verse and ask the Lord to search your heart and prepare you to respond to his promptings: "The Spirit searches all things, even the deep things of God" (1 Cor 2:10). Now focus on the day's Scripture. As you engage your heart with the suggested Scriptures and devotionals, follow the process of the acronym RIPE, as outlined below. RIPE essentially relabels, for easier recall, an ancient yet growing Christian devotional practice called *lectio divina*, which includes four phases: *lectio, meditatio, oratio* and *contemplatio*.[1]

I encourage you to write down your thoughts in a journal during these devotional exercises.

R: Read (**lectio**). Slowly read the passage several times, both silently and out loud. Make yourself aware of cultural, theological or other biases you may be bringing to the passage. Read it without allowing those biases to cloud your reading. Read it first from the viewpoint of a child who knows nothing about the cultural and theological underpinnings of the passage. After you do this, you can then bring in other background or theological insights you already know about the passage.

Take two or three minutes on this exercise.

I: Immerse (**meditatio**). Immerse yourself *in* the Scripture and ponder it by imagining yourself as one of the original hearers of this passage, physically present in a time and place in which the Scripture was spoken, written or read. Use all five senses to recreate the context and setting in your mind. Enter into the hearer's world. Center your thoughts on how the passage relates to Jesus.

Take two to three minutes on this exercise.

P: Pray (**oratio**). Pray over the Scripture and "pray the Scripture" by personalizing it for yourself. Allow the Lord to search your heart as you ponder it. Let him speak to your heart and reveal his will to you. Choose a learner's posture as you ask the Lord about what he wants to stop, start, change, develop or grow in you.

Take two to three minutes on this exercise.

E: Execute (**contemplatio**). Review what you read, what you learned as you immersed yourself in the reading and what you felt God impress on you to do. Commit to the Lord that you will carry out *today* what he has impressed on you to do, be or change. Write down what you will do. Be specific in your commitment.

Take two to three minutes on this exercise.

....

The above material simply explains the RIPE process that you will now apply to the following verses on this first day. Remember that each day you'll want to first take a few minutes completing the BEETS process to prepare yourself for the actual devotional and the RIPE process.

Now apply the RIPE process to the Scriptures below. Read the verses slowly and reflectively, silently and out loud. Immerse yourself in them. Imagine yourself in the setting in which they were written or spoken. What do you see, feel, smell or hear? Immerse yourself in the setting. Emphasize various parts of the Scripture. Especially notice the words in italics, which I have added for emphasis. As you read, pray the Scriptures and personalize them. Ask yourself how they relate to Jesus. Write down thoughts and impressions that come to mind.

As Jesus and his disciples were on their way, he came to a village where a woman named Martha opened her home to him. She had a sister called Mary, who sat at the Lord's feet *listening* to what he said. But Martha was *distracted* by all the preparations that had to be made. She came to him and asked, "Lord, don't you care that my sister has left me to do the work by myself? Tell her to help me!" "Martha, Martha," the Lord answered, "you are *worried and upset* about many things, but only *one thing is needed.* Mary has chosen what is better, and it will not be taken away from her." (Lk 10:38-42)

Finally, ask yourself what you should take away from today's devotional experience. Ask the Lord to show you what he would have you do today based on your experience in the Scripture and prayer the last few minutes.

Is he prompting you to do something at the office, in your family, with your friends or in your personal life? Do you sense his leading to change your perspective on an issue, forgive someone, make a call you've neglected, encourage someone, perform an act of service in secret, confess a sin or stop doing something? Write down what he impresses on you, and commit to doing it.

One final thought. At least once today, pause and take sixty seconds to walk mentally through the BEETS process, especially when you feel a negative emotion such as anxiety, worry, fear or anger. Ponder, reflect and pay attention to what God may be teaching you in that moment. Try to pay attention to him more frequently during each day. Seek to be fully present with him and with others more consistently.

....

That's day 1 of the BEETS/RIPE process. Instead of repeating the instructions and explanation for each of the next seven days, I've included only the Scripture, the devotional comments and a few of the instructions for the other days below. You'll do the same thing each day. Do BEETS first and then RIPE. Until it's clear in your mind, refer to the explanation I gave for BEETS and RIPE above, and go through the same process with the new Scripture and devotional thoughts.

DAY 2

Today's Scriptures focus on the biblical basis for B in BEETS.

Body: pay attention to what your body may be telling you.

So often our ministries relentlessly demand more and more from us. In our faithful attempt to meet those needs, we easily get into a hurry mode and miss living in the moment, being fully present for others and for God. We don't stop long enough to smell the roses, so to speak. Instead subtle resentment over ministry demands can cause us to either ruminate over hurts from our past or worry about the uncertainties of the future. We then busy ourselves subconsciously, hoping that our busyness will squelch unpleasant emotions or that multitasking will help us get more done.

The Bible often speaks about slowing down and physically being still before God, thus the need to practice the B in BEETS: paying attention to your body. Reflect on this quote and then the following verses about our need to stop and be still.

> Although I often try to pull it off, I know that I cannot really be present for another person when my inner world is filled with preoccupations and distractions. This is one of the biggest challenges I face in being present for others—being still within my own soul. Stillness is the precondition of presence. I must first be still to myself if I am to be still with another. And, of course, I must learn to be still before God if I am to learn to be still in myself. Presence begins with a still place within one's self. If I have no such inner place, I cannot really be present for others.[2]

Now apply the RIPE process to the Scriptures below. Read the verses slowly and reflectively, silently and out loud. Immerse yourself in them. Imagine yourself in the setting in which they were written or spoken. What do you see, feel, smell or hear? Immerse yourself in the setting. Emphasize various parts of the Scripture. Especially notice the words in italics, which I have added for emphasis. As you read, pray the Scriptures and personalize them. Ask yourself how they relate to Jesus. Write down thoughts and impressions that come to mind.

The Lord will fight for you; you need only to *be still*. (Ex 14:14)

I have stilled and quieted my soul; like a weaned child with its mother, like a weaned child is my soul within me. (Ps 131:2)

Be still before the Lord and wait patiently for him; do not fret when men succeed in their ways, when they carry out their wicked schemes. (Ps 37:7)

Be still, and know that I am God. (Ps 46:10)

Finally, ask yourself what you should take away from today's devotional experience. Ask the Lord to show you what he would have you do today based on your experience in the Scripture and prayer the last few minutes.

Is he prompting you to do something at the office, in your family, with your friends or in your personal life? Do you sense his leading to change your perspective on an issue, forgive someone, make a call you've neglected, encourage someone, perform an act of service in secret, confess a sin or stop doing something? Write down what he impresses on you, and commit to doing it.

One final thought. At least once today, pause and take sixty seconds to walk mentally through the BEETS process, especially when you feel a negative emotion such as anxiety, worry, fear or anger. Ponder, reflect and pay attention to what God may be teaching you in that moment. Try to pay attention to him more frequently during each day. Seek to be fully present with him and with others more consistently.

Day 3

Today's Scriptures focus on the biblical basis for the first E in BEETS.

Environment: pay attention to your environment and surroundings. We're often tempted to separate the secular/tangible from the spiritual/intangible. We more easily give God what we consider the spiritual aspects of our lives, like our devotional practices, ministry efforts, sermons and so on. Yet giving him the less spiritual parts of our lives often doesn't come across our radar. But Jesus never separated the secular from the spiritual. John Ortberg, a well-known pastor-writer, once said, "God is not concerned about your spiritual life; He is concerned about your entire life."

Fully following Jesus means yielding every aspect of our being to him, both the seen and the unseen, the physical and the spiritual. This implies that we can and should learn truths about spiritual realities from the world around us. The passage below on worry, part of the Sermon on the Mount, appears after Jesus' teaching about treasures on earth. Jesus tells us that we face a constant pull between trusting material things and trusting him. He puts that struggle in perspective when he says we can't serve two masters.

In that context, he immediately begins to teach about worry. To drive his point home, he encourages his listeners (and us) to look around and notice their world and learn from it. He wanted them to connect common objects in nature, like birds and flowers, to spiritual realities.

Observing and learning from our physical surroundings can help us redirect our focus from worry to confidence in him and his provision for us. But in order to learn from it, we must pay attention to it, thus the first E in BEETS: environment.

Now apply the RIPE process to the Scriptures below. Read the verses slowly and reflectively, silently and out loud. Immerse yourself in them. Imagine yourself in the setting in which they were written or spoken. What do you see, feel, smell or hear? Immerse yourself in the setting. Emphasize various parts of the Scripture. Especially notice the words in italics, which I have added for emphasis. As you read, pray the Scriptures and personalize them. Ask yourself how they relate to Jesus. Write down thoughts and impressions that come to mind.

Therefore I tell you, do not worry about your life, what you will eat or drink; or about your body, what you will wear. Is not life more important than food, and the body more important than clothes? *Look at the birds of the air; they do not sow or reap or store away in barns,* and yet your heavenly Father feeds them. Are you not much more valuable than they? Who of you by worrying can add a single hour to his life? And why do you worry about clothes? *See how the lilies of the field grow. They do not labor or spin.* Yet I tell you that not even Solomon in all his splendor was dressed like one of these. If that is how God clothes the grass of the field, which is here today and tomorrow is thrown into the fire, will he not much more clothe you, O you of little faith? *So do not worry, saying, "What shall we eat?" or "What shall we drink?" or "What shall we wear?"* For the pagans run after all these things, and your heavenly Father knows that you need them. But *seek first his kingdom* and his righteousness, and all these things will be given to you as well. Therefore do not worry about tomorrow, for tomorrow will worry about itself. Each day has enough trouble of its own. (Mt 6:25-34)

Finally, ask yourself what you should take away from today's devotional experience. Ask the Lord to show you what he would have you do today based on your experience in the Scripture and prayer the last few minutes.

Is he prompting you to do something at the office, in your family, with your friends or in your personal life? Do you sense his leading to change your perspective on an issue, forgive someone, make a call you've neglected, encourage someone, perform an act of service in secret, confess a sin or stop doing something? Write down what he impresses on you, and commit to doing it.

One final thought. At least once today, pause and take sixty seconds to walk mentally through the BEETS process, especially when you feel a negative emotion such as anxiety, worry, fear or anger. Ponder, reflect and pay attention to what God may be teaching you in that moment. Try to pay attention to him more frequently during each day. Seek to be fully present with him and with others more consistently.

DAY 4

Today's Scriptures focus on the biblical basis for the second E in BEETS.

Emotions: pay attention to your emotions and feelings.

One of the gifts God has given us humans is our emotional life. Without it, life would be dull and colorless. We love the good emotions and try to avoid the bad ones. Yet God often speaks through the bad ones. C. S. Lewis wrote, "God whispers to us in our pleasures, speaks to us in our conscience, but shouts in our pains: It is His megaphone to rouse a deaf world."

Emotions are an important way God can connect to our hearts. When the unpleasant ones come, however, we often attempt to suppress them instead of learning and growing from them.

Now apply the RIPE process to the quotes below. Read the verses slowly and reflectively, silently and out loud. Immerse yourself in them. Imagine yourself in the setting in which they were written or spoken. What do you see, feel, smell or hear? Immerse yourself in the setting. Emphasize various parts of the Scripture. Especially notice the words in italics, which I have added for emphasis. As you read, pray the Scriptures and personalize them. Ask yourself how they relate to Jesus. Write down thoughts and impressions that come to mind.

> Ignoring our emotions is turning our back on reality; listening to our emotions ushers us into reality. And reality is where we meet God. . . . Emotions are the language of the soul. They are the cry that gives the heart a voice. . . . However,

we often turn a deaf ear—through emotional denial, distortion, or disengagement. We strain out anything disturbing in order to gain tenuous control of our inner world. We are frightened and ashamed of what leaks into our consciousness. In neglecting our intense emotions, we are false to ourselves and lose a wonderful opportunity to know God. We forget that change comes through brutal honesty and vulnerability before God.[3]

Trust in him at all times, O people; *pour out your hearts* to him, for God is our refuge. (Ps 62:8)

When Mary reached the place where Jesus was and saw him, she fell at his feet and said, "Lord, if you had been here, my brother would not have died." When Jesus saw her weeping, and the Jews who had come along with her also weeping, *he was deeply moved in spirit and troubled.* "Where have you laid him?" he asked. "Come and see, Lord," they replied. *Jesus wept.* Then the Jews said, "See how he loved him!" (Jn 11:32-36)

Until now you have not asked for anything in my name. Ask and you will receive, and your *joy* will be complete. (Jn 16:24)

For the kingdom of God is not a matter of eating and drinking, but of righteousness, *peace and joy* in the Holy Spirit. (Rom 14:17)

Finally, ask yourself what you should take away from today's devotional experience. Ask the Lord to show you what he would have you do today based on your experience in the Scripture and prayer the last few minutes.

Is he prompting you to do something at the office, in your family, with your friends or in your personal life? Do you sense his leading to change your perspective on an issue, forgive someone, make a call you've neglected, encourage someone, perform an act of service in secret, confess a sin or stop doing something? Write down what he impresses on you, and commit to doing it.

One final thought. At least once today, pause and take sixty seconds to walk mentally through the BEETS process, especially when you feel a negative emotion such as anxiety, worry, fear or anger. Ponder, reflect and pay attention to what God may be teaching you in that moment. Try to pay attention to him more frequently during each day. Seek to be fully present with him and with others more consistently.

DAY 5

Today's Scriptures focus on the biblical basis for the T in BEETS.

Thoughts: pay attention to what you are thinking about.

Your mind and brain is an amazing God-created part of your body. While comprising only 2 to 3 percent of your body's total body weight, it takes 20 percent of its energy because it serves as your body's command and control center. The word *mind* appears more than 160 times in the Bible, and the mind is central to our spiritual growth.

A spiritually and emotionally healthy mind helps us in several ways. It helps us pay attention to what is important to God, to learn spiritual truth, to regulate our emotions and to remember biblical truth. Unfortunately, our minds often wander into unprofitable and even sinful thinking. Perhaps that's why Paul lists several wholesome qualities in Philippians 4:8 we should focus our thinking on.

One way we can ensure we are thinking rightly is to check in on our own thoughts periodically, thus the T in BEETS, which stands for paying attention to our thoughts. In other words, we need to think about what we are thinking about so that, if necessary, we can replace unprofitable thinking with wholesome thinking. The more frequently we intentionally become aware of our thoughts and declutter our minds, the more we will position ourselves to sense the Spirit's gentle promptings.

Now apply the RIPE process to the quotes below. Read the verses slowly and reflectively, silently and out loud. Immerse yourself in them. Imagine yourself in the setting in which they were written or spoken. What do you see, feel, smell or hear? Immerse yourself in the setting. Emphasize various parts of the Scripture. Especially notice the words in italics, which I have added for emphasis. As you read, pray the Scriptures and personalize them. Ask yourself how they relate to Jesus. Write down thoughts and impressions that come to mind.

> When I am still, compulsion (the busyness that Hilary of Tours called "a blasphemous anxiety to do God's work for him") gives way to compunction (being pricked or punctured). That is, God can break through the many layers with which I protect myself, so that I can hear His Word and be poised to listen. . . .
>
> I can mistake the flow of my adrenaline for the moving of the Holy Spirit; I can live in the illusion that I am ultimately in control of my destiny and my daily affairs.
>
> Blaise Pascal observed that most of our human problems come because we don't know how to sit still in our room for an hour.[4]

> The boy Samuel ministered before the LORD under Eli. In those days the word of the LORD was rare; there were not many visions. One night Eli, whose eyes were becoming so weak that he could barely see, was lying down in his usual place. The lamp of God had not yet gone out, and Samuel was lying down in the temple of the LORD, where the ark of God was.
>
> Then the LORD called Samuel. Samuel answered, "Here I am." And he ran to Eli and said, "Here I am; you called me."

But Eli said, "I did not call; go back and lie down." So he went and lay down.

Again the LORD called, "Samuel!" And Samuel got up and went to Eli and said, "Here I am; you called me." "My son," Eli said, "I did not call; go back and lie down."

Now Samuel did not yet know the LORD: The word of the LORD had not yet been revealed to him. The LORD called Samuel a third time, and Samuel got up and went to Eli and said, "Here I am; you called me." Then Eli realized that the LORD was calling the boy.

So Eli told Samuel, *"Go and lie down, and if he calls you, say, 'Speak, LORD, for your servant is listening.'"* So Samuel went and lay down in his place. The LORD came and stood there, calling as at the other times, "Samuel! Samuel!" Then Samuel said, *"Speak, for your servant is listening."* (1 Sam 3:1-10).

Finally, ask yourself what you should take away from today's devotional experience. Ask the Lord to show you what he would have you do today based on your experience in the Scripture and prayer the last few minutes.

Is he prompting you to do something at the office, in your family, with your friends or in your personal life? Do you sense his leading to change your perspective on an issue, forgive someone, make a call you've neglected, encourage someone, perform an act of service in secret, confess a sin or stop doing something? Write down what he impresses on you, and commit to doing it.

One final thought. At least once today, pause and take sixty seconds to walk mentally through the BEETS process, especially when you feel a negative emotion such as anxiety, worry, fear or anger. Ponder, reflect and pay attention to what God may be teaching you in that moment. Try to pay attention to him more frequently during each day. Seek to be fully present with him and with others more consistently.

DAY 6

Today's Scriptures focus on the biblical basis for the S in BEETS.

Soul: pay attention to your soul.

Most pastors would agree that we should pay attention to our souls, our spiritual lives. When we came to faith, God forgave us based on Jesus' work on the cross. He gave us a new heart and sealed us with his Spirit. He promised never to leave or forsake us. And he gave us the promise of eternal life in heaven. As a result, we should practice spiritual disciplines to help us grow in our faith and love him more. We read, study and teach God's Word. We pray when we're alone and when we're with others. Many practice other disciplines as well, such as fasting, solitude, mindfulness and silence. Most of us need little convincing to grow our souls.

However, I've found that we seldom consider how profoundly our bodies, our environments, our emotions and our thoughts affect our soul development. The first four steps of BEETS are meant to place our total being into the best possible position for God to work in our souls. They are meant to help create internal space, clear our mental deck and focus our attention on him.

Now apply the RIPE process to the quotes below. Read the verses slowly and reflectively, silently and out loud. Immerse yourself in them. Imagine yourself in the setting in which they were written or spoken. What do you see, feel, smell or hear? Immerse yourself in the setting. Emphasize various parts of the Scripture. Especially notice the words in italics, which I have added for emphasis. As you read, pray the Scriptures and personalize them. Ask yourself how they relate to Jesus. Write down thoughts and impressions that come to mind.

Each of us needs an opportunity to be alone, and silent, to find space in the day or in the week, just to reflect and to listen to the voice of God that speaks deep within us. Our search for God is our only response to his search for us. He knocks at our door, but for many people their lives are too preoccupied for them to be able to hear.[5]

He replied, "I have been very zealous for the LORD God Almighty. The Israelites have rejected your covenant, broken down your altars, and put your prophets to death with the sword. I am the only one left, and now they are trying to kill me too." The LORD said, "Go out and stand on the mountain in the presence of the LORD, for the LORD is about to pass by." Then a great and powerful wind tore the mountains apart and shattered the rocks before the LORD, but the LORD was not in the wind. After the wind there was an earthquake, but the LORD was not in the earthquake. After the earthquake came a fire, but the LORD was not in the fire. And after the fire came a *gentle whisper*. When Elijah heard it, he pulled his cloak over his face and went out and stood at the mouth of the cave. (1 Kings 19:10-13)

Finally, ask yourself what you should take away from today's devotional experience. Ask the Lord to show you what he would have you do today based on your experience in the Scripture and prayer the last few minutes.

Is he prompting you to do something at the office, in your family, with your friends or in your personal life? Do you sense his leading to change your perspective on an issue, forgive someone, make a call you've neglected, encourage someone, perform an act of service in secret, confess a sin or stop doing something? Write down what he impresses on you, and commit to doing it.

One final thought. At least once today, pause and take sixty seconds to walk mentally through the BEETS process, especially when you feel a negative emotion such as anxiety, worry, fear or anger. Ponder, reflect and pay attention to what God may be teaching you in that moment. Try to pay attention to him more frequently during each day. Seek to be fully present with him and with others more consistently.

DAY 7

Day 7 does not include any new Scriptures. On this day, go back and review days 1-6 and pick one set of Scriptures that resonated with you. Then use the BEETS/RIPE process with those.

....

Seven days won't make a habit. However, if you used the BEETS/RIPE process during the last seven days, you are familiar enough to apply the process to your devotions during the next few weeks. I encourage you to do that and discover how mindfulness can help you become more of a PRESENT leader.

*THE EIGHT-WEEK TEAM
DEVELOPMENT PLAN*

None of us is as smart as all of us.

KEN BLANCHARD

*The ratio of We's to I's is the best
indicator of the development of a team.*

LEWIS B. ERGEN

Chapter snapshot. In this chapter I suggest an eight-week plan
you can use to build the PRESENT principles into your staff, leadership teams, boards and volunteers in eight twenty- to thirty-
minute sessions. It can also be used as a personal development
guide. When used with a group, I suggest that each team member read the corresponding chapter(s) before each session and
complete any related inventories or assignments beforehand.
One way to make the learning stick is to let each member lead
part of a session. Each weekly lesson includes five sections: a
summary of the related chapter's content, a case study for discussion, questions to discuss in the group, a next step(s) and a
reminder about the tool recommended in that chapter.

Week 1: The People Pleaser Versus the PRESENT Leader (Introduction–Chapter 3)

Summary. Unhealthy people pleasing is a common leadership problem among today's pastors, affecting over 70 percent to some degree. Since it acts much like a virus, it takes a strong leadership *immune system* to counter it. By incorporating insight from the Bible, family systems and neuroscience, a pastor can develop a healthy immune system.

Rooted in the immature ways we handle our ongoing negative emotions (chronic anxiety), people pleasing is mostly driven by the emotional parts of our brains rather than the thinking parts. When we grow our emotional maturity (what family systems theory calls differentiation of self) in both our inner world (thinking and feeling) and our outer world (individuality and connectedness), we are less apt to people please. We grow our maturity by developing others and ourselves into PRESENT leaders instead of pleaser leaders.

Case study. Pretend this is true in your church. A middle-aged man attends who went to seminary twenty years prior, yet quit halfway through his degree. He now works as a history teacher in the local high school. He knows enough theology to make him "dangerous." He often sends you an email or confronts you after the service to correct you about a theological point or to suggest that you make a change in your sermon delivery.

You've tried to accommodate his suggestions for several months, even though you disagree with most of them. His comments have now become more critical. Every time you see his name in your email inbox or notice him in the congregation when you preach, your heart jumps and you feel anxious. His criticism is affecting your confidence and your leadership. Based on these chapters, what is one step you could take to lessen your pleaser tendencies toward him and lower your anxiety?

Questions. When you took the self-evaluation quiz in chapter 1, were you surprised at your score? Why or why not? What stood out?

Which of the stories from pastors in chapter 1 did you most resonate with? Why?

What might clue you to chronic anxiety in your life or leadership? Take a few moments and review this list to discover if you have any of these traits.

- I can mindlessly yield to others' opinions to avoid more anxiety.

- I sometimes blow up at others too easily.

- I tend to focus on others' reactions and responses to me.

- I can be easily and quickly hurt.

- I often see myself as a victim.

- I resort to either/or, yes/no or black/white thinking.

- I sometimes cast blame or falsely criticize others.

- I often entertain threats from others (for example, "I'm going to leave the church unless you . . .").

Next steps. What is one simple step you can take next week to change one of you pleaser behaviors?

Tools. None are provided for these chapters; however, in question 1 above you revisited the self-evaluation quiz in chapter 1. Consider reviewing your results with your team.

Week 2: Probe Your Past (Chapter 4)

Summary. People-pleasing tendencies often come from thinking, feeling and relating scripts we learned in our family of origin. Connecting with our families and creating a family diagram can help us uncover both unhealthy and healthy patterns. Understanding those tendencies can help free us from pleaser tendencies.

Case study. You've had a good relationship with those on your board. But recently you added a new member who seems to take issue with every proposal you bring. You've heard that he had a difficult childhood. You suspect that he's bringing some of his childhood issues into your meetings. How could you discover if your hunch is right? If you find you are right, how could you best deal with this issue during meetings?

Questions. Does creating a genogram resonate with you? Do you see value in it? Why or why not?

What's a first step you can take to begin creating a family diagram?

Next steps. Create your own family diagram, and share it with your team. Encourage them to do the same. Schedule a time when you all share what you learned from your family diagram.

As a team, create a family diagram of your church and significant leaders.

Tools. The family diagram, also called a genogram. You'll find many online resources that can help you create a family and church genogram. I recommended the short yet thorough book *A Family Genogram Workbook* by Israel Galindo, Elaine Boomer and Don Reagan.

WEEK 3: REVISIT YOUR VALUES (CHAPTER 5)

Summary. Great leaders lead from the inside out. They've developed strong core convictions that guide their leadership. Pastors can best define their true identity when they clarify their deeply held values (called gyrocompass values in chapter 4). As a result pastors will act from conviction rather than from emotion when they face church pressures.

Case study. A pastor wrote this true story.

I have a youth minister who is over-the-top sensitive, to the point she will cry right in the pulpit. At the bare minimum, she wears a pouting look on her face for the remainder of the service if I correct her for whatever reason. This has affected me because I feel like I must walk on eggshells around her. I don't want to see her cry. I'm sometimes more conscious about avoiding hurting her feelings instead of telling her the truth or correcting her (which I know is not good). Her sad countenance and hurt feelings cause her to pull away, even while she is in your presence.

Since she is a leader, it distracts the members when they see her sad countenance during our worship service. I try to ignore it when I'm preaching, but there she is with that sad look on her face. No matter what I do to help her get over it, she doesn't respond. She tends to stay in that state for a few weeks at a time. My only response now is to minimize my exposure to her when she acts like that.

In light of this chapter, what would you do if you were in his shoes?

Questions. Who in your circle of influence best models gyrocompass values? What about that person made you think of him or her?

What kind of ministry circumstances most often push against your gyrocompass values?

Next steps. Talk with your team about scheduling a half-day retreat when members can explore their values.

Tools. The gyrocompass values retreat process.

WEEK 4: EXPOSE YOUR TRIANGLES (CHAPTER 6)

Summary. Triangles are the essential building blocks relationships are built on. They are the way people handle their anxious emotions. For a leader to counter people pleasing and lead well, he must think in threes by making himself aware of the triangles around him, and he must learn to respond appropriately to unhealthy ones.

Case study. Pastor Mike comes to his new church and nine months later learns that a longstanding member is questioning his leadership behind his back. She hasn't talked with him about this personally.

Rather, she has met with five other influential members of the church to share her concerns, two of whom told the pastor about the conversations. This situation has put the pastor into five unhealthy triangles as an "excluded one." Given the insights you learned from this chapter, if you were Pastor Mike, what would you do?

Questions. Think about your family when you grew up. What kinds of triangles were you in? How did you act in them?

Compare the dynamics in your family triangles to the ones you're now in. What similarities do you see in how you acted then and now?

Next steps. Have your team take five minutes to quickly draw the most prominent triangles they're in. Have them classify each one as healthy or unhealthy and explain why.

Tools. The list of tips in chapter 6 on how to learn from and expose unhealthy triangles.

Week 5: Search for Your Gaps (Chapter 7)

Summary. We all have weaknesses and blind spots. Without fixating on them, a good leader will become aware of hers and seek to address them. Leaders must become more self-aware to notice such growth opportunities. Based on family systems, six gaps can indicate people pleasing: emotional reactivity, fusion, emotional cutoff, not taking an I-position, overfunctioning and underfunctioning.

Case study. Pastor Fred has been at his church for five years and has repeatedly experienced tension with his board. When they meet, the tension hinders thoughtful discussion and clouds the decision making necessary to move the church forward. As a result, the church is stuck in a holding pattern.

You've been asked to consult with the board and the pastor to help. It doesn't take long for you to see several gaps in the leadership and to conclude that those gaps have made the meetings unproductive. How would you broach the subject of gaps? And what steps would you suggest to help them address the gaps to make their meetings productive so they can make good decisions to help move the church forward?

Questions. Have each team member take and score the short-form DSI before you meet. You can find it at the web link under "Tools" below. When you meet, ask everyone to share their results and how they compared to the 1,200 pastors in the study (composite scores below). Were you surprised at what you discovered? Why or why not? Remember, the higher the scores, the healthier you are in that area.

- Emotional reactivity: 4.1

- Lack of I-position: 4.4

- Emotional cutoff: 4.8

- Fusion: 4.2

Think about the lowest average score—emotional reactivity—and rate the emotional reactivity of your own key leaders. If it's a problem in your church, what are some steps you could take that could help your leaders grow in that area?

Next steps. Ask your team to reflect on its lowest score during the following week and to develop a simple action plan for personal growth.

Tools. The DSI. Find it at this web link: https://mospace.umsystem .edu/xmlui/bitstream/handle/10355/11137/DrakeDifSelInv.pdf.

WEEK 6: ENGAGE YOUR CRITICS (CHAPTER 8)

Summary. When people criticize, hassle or otherwise resist us in ministry, we naturally shy away from them. Actually, staying in reasonable contact with them may help decrease tension. Good leaders don't distance themselves from their critics. Rather, they learn to relate to them with a calm presence. However, staying in contact does not imply that we allow ourselves to be emotionally or verbally abused by them.

Case study. Todd, a senior pastor friend at a neighboring church, asks you to have lunch with him. He wants your wisdom on how to respond to a blowup in a recent elders' meeting at his church. You meet, and among the many issues he shares is this scenario: The lead elder, whose son was recently divorced, has been distancing himself from Todd. At one time they would meet monthly for breakfast to discuss ministry issues and build rapport. However, the past two months the elder has cancelled breakfast at the last minute. At the last elders' meeting, he surprised Todd by vehemently opposing a plan to fill the vacant youth pastor slot, citing the economy's potential drag on giving. What advice would you give Todd in light of this chapter?

Questions. With what person in the church have you experienced the most conflict? Based on insights from this chapter, what can you do differently from now on, if anything?

How have you created a leadership culture in your ministry that encourages differing viewpoints and unpleasant emotions to be appropriately brought out in the open?

How do you deal with critical people and dissidents? Who in your circle of influence that you trust could give you objective feedback on how you deal with critics?

Next steps. Ask the team members to pray for their critics in the following week. Ask them to ask a trusted friend or a family member to share how he or she feels that team member handles criticism.

Tools. The list in chapter 8 on ways to engage critics.

WEEK 7: NURTURE YOUR SOUL (CHAPTER 9)

Summary. Genuine soul care often takes a back seat in a busy pastor's life. While most pastors have quiet times, most don't practice a discipline modeled by some of the greatest saints in the past— that is, mindfulness, being fully present in the moment for God and others. Mindfulness helps us declutter our minds so that by being more consistently aware of our thoughts, we can more often think the thoughts that Jesus wants us to think. Mindfulness gives us the ability to live in the moment while disengaging from automatic thoughts, feelings, memories and reactions.

Case study. Let's assume that you want to begin practicing mindfulness. After a few weeks of practicing it, you find it's been very helpful. You want to introduce the concept to your board so they can experience its benefits. The day after you explain the concept, you get a strongly worded email from a board member who says you're using Buddhist/New Age philosophy that contradicts the Bible. How would you respond to such a critic? What evidence could you use to help him see the biblical basis of Christian mindfulness?

Questions. Was this concept of mindfulness new to you? How could it fit into your spiritual toolbox to help you grow?

Do you think Brother Lawrence's experience of living in the conscious moment-by-moment presence of the Lord is realistic in today's fast-paced world? Why or why not? How could you adapt it to your world?

Next steps. If your team has never read Brother Lawrence's book, *The Practice of the Presence of God*, encourage them to download or buy a copy and read it. You can find ebook downloads for free on some sites and for a nominal price on others.

Tools. The BEETS plan.

Week 8: Tame Your Reactivity (Chapter 10)

Summary. According to my research, emotional reactivity is a common weakness among pastors. We often let our emotions reflexively dictate our responses when under pressure, which often makes matters worse. However, neuroscience is now giving us clues about practical ways we can stay cool under pressure. With the Holy Spirit's help, we can quiet the emotional parts of our brains through three reflective responses: label the emotion, reappraise the situation and self-distance.

Case study. Reread the story about Pastor John in the first part of chapter 10. Given the content of that chapter, if you faced what he did, would you have taken the same approach in dealing with the critical board member? If not, what would you have done differently?

Questions. Revisit the transformer metaphor. Have you ever been in a setting when someone acted like a step-up transformer? What happened to the group or family dynamics when that person ramped up his or her emotions?

On the other side of the coin, have you ever been in an emotional meeting when the leader acted like a step-down transformer? What did that leader do to bring down the group's emotional temperature?

Next steps. Ask your team to take note the following week when something or someone tempts them to let their emotions dictate a response. Have them note the emotional regulation strategy they used. Ask them to be prepared the next time you meet to share what they did.

Tools. The three emotional strategies: label, reappraise, self-distance.

I BASED THIS BOOK'S RESEARCH on three different surveys. For the *first survey*, I hired LifeWay Research to survey 1,002 pastors in January of 2011 via telephone interviews. The calling list was randomly drawn from a list of all Protestant churches, and the sample provided 95 percent confidence that the error would not exceed +/- 3.2 percent. This survey included these three questions in addition to several about demographics:

1. How often do you make decisions in your ministry that are motivated by a desire to appease or please someone else, gain their approval or avoid conflict?

2. There are often regrettable consequences to making decisions in your ministry that are motivated by the desire to appease or please someone else, gain their approval or avoid conflict. (Participants were instructed to "select all that apply" from six options.)

3. Have you experienced any of the following difficulties as the result of a decision you made that was motivated by your desire to appease or please someone else, gain their approval or avoid conflict? Select all that apply. (Six options plus a "none" were provided.)

The *second survey* was an online questionnaire given to three groups of pastors in August, September and November of 2011. A total of 1,910 surveys were taken with 1,246 used in the analysis. The respondents came from three sources: Christianity Today's *Preaching Today* newsletter subscribers, Outreach's Churchleaders .com newsletter subscribers and a targeted group of Latino pastors in Central and South America.

This survey included the same three questions as the LifeWay survey plus an extensive survey called the Differentiation of Self Inventory[1] that examined differentiation of self, a Bowen Family Systems concept that describes certain aspects of personal maturity. The margin of error based on this sample size was +/-2.8 percent, 95 percent of the time, on questions where opinion was evenly split (50 percent).

DETAILS PER SURVEY

1. August survey
   - Surveys accepted from August 25 to September 5, 2011
   - Total surveys started: 1,108
   - Total surveys completed: 826
   - Survey invitations: sent to CT's *Preaching Today* newsletter
   - Incentive: respondents were invited to enter a drawing for one (1) iPad

2. September survey
   - Surveys accepted from September 30 to November 22, 2011
   - Total surveys started: 108
   - Total surveys completed: 56
   - Survey invitations: respondents from August survey redirected to this survey after the August survey was closed
   - Incentive: iPad

3. November survey

- Surveys accepted from November 18 to May 7, 2012
- Total surveys started: 694
- Total surveys completed: 364
- Survey invitations: sent to Outreach's ChurchLeaders.com newsletter
- Incentive: respondents were invited to enter a drawing for one (1) Kindle Fire

The margin of error based on this sample size was +/-2.8 percent, 95 percent of the time, on questions where opinion was evenly split (50 percent). Margin of error is higher when data is reported by subgroups. As the sample size decreases, the margin of error increases.

The *third survey* was a pre- to post-analysis testing the impact of focused devotions that included a mindfulness exercise called BEETS (see appendix A for a detailed explanation of BEETS). The research project was conducted from October 29 to November 19, 2012.

The research process included the following three phases.

Pre-Questionnaire Inventory

- The DSI short form was used in both the pre- and post-inventory. The short form used twenty questions instead of forty-six to make it easier to take. The short form was tested to be sufficiently valid and reliable across all four sub-scales.[2]
- Surveys accepted from October 29 to November 2, 2012.
- An email invitation was sent to 1,722 of Charles Stone's blog subscribers.
- Total surveys completed: 165.

Seven-Day Devotional Experience

- 155 of the participants were sent BEETS devotionals.

- 10 of the participants were sent general devotionals, without BEETS, as a control group.

- Devotionals were sent the morning of November 6-9 and 12-14. A reminder was sent in the afternoon to those who did not open the devotional. A separate BEETS reminder was sent to the BEETS group.

Post-Questionnaire Survey

- Surveys were accepted from November 15-19, 2012.

- Total surveys completed: 87 with BEETS, 7 without BEETS.

- Incentive: respondents were invited to enter a drawing for one (1) iPad mini.

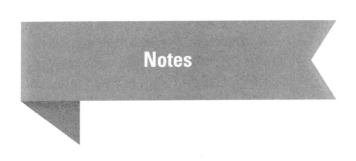

Notes

Introduction: My Personal Confession

[1]Edwin H. Friedman, *A Failure of Nerve: Leadership in the Age of the Quick Fix* (Bethesda, MD: Friedman Estate, 1999), p. 19.

[2]Ibid., p. 18.

[3]Harriet B. Braiker, *The Disease to Please: Curing the People-Pleasing Syndrome* (New York: McGraw-Hill, 2001), p. 48.

[4]For more information, see "Murray Bowen, M.D.," Bowen Theory, www .thebowencenter.org/pages/murraybowen.html.

Chapter 1: Has the People-Pleaser Virus Infected Your Leadership?

[1]Susan Cain, *Quiet: The Power of Introverts in a World That Can't Stop Talking* (New York: Random House, 2012), p. 21.

[2]Ibid., pp. 22-23.

[3]Quoted in Eric Landry, "From a Movement to a Church: Part 3," Out of the Horse's Mouth: The White Horse Inn Blog, November 20, 2009, www .whitehorseinn.org/blog/2009/11/30/from-a-movement-to-a-church -part-3/.

[4]Edwin H. Friedman, *A Failure of Nerve: Leadership in the Age of the Quick Fix* (Bethesda, MD: Friedman Estate, 1999), p. 139.

[5]Quoted in Peter L. Steinke, *How Your Church Family Works: Understanding Congregations as Emotional Systems* (Herndon, VA: The Alban Institute, 2006), Kindle ebook, loc. 1057.

Chapter 2: What Makes Leaders Sick?

[1]Rob Schrepfer, "From the Leadership Development Cabinet Desk," Duke Leadership Development Initiative, accessed December 24, 2012, https:// mbaa.fuqua.duke.edu/ldi/press_wagdodge.html.

[2]Harriet B. Braiker, *The Disease to Please: Curing the People-Pleasing Syndrome* (New York: McGraw-Hill, 2001), p. 10.

[3]Peter L. Steinke, *Congregational Leadership in Anxious Times: Being Calm and Courageous No Matter What* (Herndon, VA: The Alban Institute, 2006), p. 7.

[4]James Rapson and Craig English, *Anxious to Please: 7 Revolutionary Practices for the Chronically Nice* (Naperville, IL: Sourcebooks, 2006), Kindle ebook, loc. 383.

[5]Kevin Cashman, *Leadership from the Inside Out: Becoming a Leader for Life* (San Francisco: Berrett-Koehler Publishers, 2008), Kindle ebook, loc. 428.

[6]Steinke, *Congregational Leadership*, p. 146.

[7]Peter Steinke, *How Your Church Family Works: Understanding Congregations as Emotional Systems* (Herndon, VA: The Alban Institute), Kindle ebook, loc. 354-67.

[8]Edwin H. Friedman, *A Failure of Nerve: Leadership in the Age of the Quick Fix* (Bethesda, MD: Friedman Estate, 1999), pp. 53-54.

[9]Peter L. Steinke, "Clergy Affairs," *Journal of Psychology and Christianity* 8, no. 4 (1989): 61.

[10]Ibid., p. 62.

Chapter 3: The Key to Health: A Strong Leadership Immune System

[1]"Dr. Semmelweis' Biography," Semmelweis Society International, accessed December 24, 2013, http://semmelweis.org/about/dr-semmelweis-biography/.

[2]Special thanks to Emyln Ott, assistant professor of ministry and pastoral leadership at Trinity Lutheran Seminary in Columbus, Ohio, and chief executive officer and director of Healthy Congregations in Columbus, Ohio, for allowing me to use her definitions.

[3]Roberta Gilbert, *The Cornerstone Concept* (Falls Church, VA: Leading Systems Press, 2008).

[4]Murray Bowen, *Family Therapy in Clinical Practice* (New York: Aronson, 1978), p. 365.

Chapter 4: The Rearview Mirror Look: Probe Your Past

[1]Edwin H. Friedman, *A Failure of Nerve: Leadership in the Age of the Quick Fix* (Bethesda, MD: Friedman Estate, 1999), p. 249.

[2]Peter Scazzero, *Emotionally Healthy Spirituality* (Nashville: Thomas Nelson, 2006), Kindle ebook, loc. 995.

[3]Ibid., loc. 975.

[4]Margaret J. Marcuson, *Leaders Who Last: Sustaining Yourself and Your Ministry* (New York: Seabury Books, 2009), Kindle ebook, loc. 403.

[5]Ronald W. Richardson, *Becoming a Healthier Pastor* (Minneapolis: Fortress, 2005), p. 61.

[6]Friedman, *A Failure of Nerve*, p. 199.

Chapter 5: The Search Within: Revisit Your Values

[1]John Ortberg, *The Life You've Always Wanted* (Grand Rapids: Zondervan, 1997), p. 152.

[2]Gary McIntosh and Samuel Rima, *Overcoming the Dark Side of Leadership* (Grand Rapids: Baker Books, 2007), Kindle ebook, loc. 1176.

[3]Lawrence Matthews, "Leadership: Viewed Through a Family Systems Lens," Leadership in Ministry Workshops, accessed November 15, 2012, www .leadershipinministry.org/resources/articles-and-other-resources/leadership -bfs-lens.

[4]Mark C. Crowley, "The Leadership Genius of Abraham Lincoln," *Fast Company*, November 9, 2012, www.fastcompany.com/3002803/leadership -genius-abraham-lincoln.

Chapter 6: When Relationships Get All Knotted Up: Expose Your Triangles

[1]Margaret J. Marcuson, *Leaders Who Last: Sustaining Yourself and Your Ministry* (New York: Seabury Books, 2009), Kindle ebook, loc. 645.

[2]Tom Hay, "Coming Back Energized from a Sabbatical," unpublished presentation at Eastern Mennonite University, Extraordinary Leadership Seminar, June 2006.

[3]Marcuson, *Leaders Who Last,* loc. 582.

Chapter 7: What's Missing: Search for Your Gaps

[1]William J. Horvat, "The Attack on Pearl Harbor," Hawaii Aviation, accessed December 24, 2012, http://hawaii.gov/hawaiiaviation/world-war-ii/december-7-1941.

[2]Bill George, "Leadership Skills Start with Self-Awareness," blog, February 28, 2011, www.billgeorge.org/page/leadership-skills-start-with-self-awareness.

[3]Baltasar Gracián, *The Art of Worldly Wisdom* (1647), maxim 69; www.terra quote.com/by/baltasar-gracin/.

[4]Elizabeth Skowron and Myrna L. Friedlander, "The Differentiation of Self Inventory: Development and Initial Validation," *Journal of Counseling Psychology* 45, no. 3 (1998): 235-46.

[5]Oscar Wilde, *De Profundis* (1905); www.quotationspage.com/quote/39782.html.

[6]Robert Gilbert, *The Cornerstone Concept* (Falls Church, VA: Leading Systems Press, 2008), p. 232.

[7]Gregory S. Burns et al., "Neurobiological Correlates of Social Conformity

and Independence During Mental Rotation," *Biological Psychiatry* 58 (2005): 245-53.

Chapter 8: Nitpickers and Stone Throwers: Engage Your Critics

[1]Dennis N. T. Perkins, *Leading on the Edge* (New York: AMACOM, 2000), p. 6.

[2]Margaret J. Marcuson, *Leaders Who Last: Sustaining Yourself and Your Ministry* (New York: Seabury Books, 2009), Kindle ebook, loc. 1117, emphasis added.

[3]Ibid., loc. 1182.

[4]I drew facts about Shackleton from Marcuson, *Leaders Who Last,* and Perkins, *Leading on the Edge.*

[5]Perkins, *Leading on the Edge*, p. 111.

[6]Edwin H. Friedman, *A Failure of Nerve: Leadership in the Age of the Quick Fix* (Bethesda, MD: Friedman Estate, 1999), p. 214.

[7]Marcuson, *Leaders Who Last,* loc. 815.

[8]Roberta Gilbert, *Extraordinary Leadership: Thinking Systems Make a Difference* (Falls Church, VA: Leading Systems Press, 2009), p. 136.

[9]Marcuson, *Leaders Who Last,* loc. 1132.

[10]Travis Bradberry and Jean Greaves, *Emotional Intelligence 2.0* (San Diego: TalentSmart, 2009), Kindle ebook, loc. 630.

[11]Friedman, *A Failure of Nerve*, p. 229.

[12]Bradbury and Greaves, *Emotional Intelligence 2.0,* loc. 1886.

[13]Perkins, *Leading on the Edge*, p. 111.

[14]Edwin Friedman, *Generation to Generation* (New York: The Guilford Press, 1985), p. 210.

[15]Christopher Page, "A Non-Anxious Presence," *In a Spacious Place*, June 4, 2009, http://inaspaciousplace.blogspot.com/2009/06/non-anxious-presence .html.

Chapter 9: Self-Care: Nurture Your Soul through Mindfulness

[1]"About Brother Lawrence of the Resurrection," *Blog by the Sea*, March 17, 2006, http://blog-by-the-sea.typepad.com/blog_bythesea/2006/03/about_brother _l.html.

[2]Brother Lawrence, *The Practice of the Presence of God*, Kindle ebook, loc. 40.

[3]Ibid., loc. 253.

[4]Ibid., loc. 469.

[5]Ibid., loc. 546.

[6]Daniel J. Siegel, *Pocket Guide to Interpersonal Neurobiology* (New York: Norton, 2012), p. 40.

[7]Stefan Hoffman, "The Effect of Mindfulness-Based Therapy on Anxiety and

Depression," *Journal of Consulting and Clinical Psychology* 78, no. 2 (April 2010): 169-83.

[8]David Rock, *Your Brain at Work* (New York: Harper Collins, 2009), p. 87.

[9]Ibid., p. 92.

Chapter 10: Are Your Reactions Showing? Tame Your Reactivity

[1]Peter I. Steinke, *How Your Church Family Works: Understanding Congregations As Emotional Systems* (Herndon, VA: The Alban Institute, 2006), p. 18.

[2]Matthew Lieberman, "The Brain's Braking System," accessed December 26, 2012, www.scn.ucla.edu/pdf/Lieberman(InPress)Neuroleadership.pdf.

[3]Lieberman, Matthew, et al., "Putting Feelings into Words: Affect Labeling Disrupts Amygdala Activity in Response to Affective Stimuli," *Psychological Science* 18, no. 5 (2007): 421-28.

[4]P. R. Goldin et al., "The Neural Bases of Emotion Regulation: Reappraisal and Suppression of Negative Emotion," *Biological Psychiatry* 63, no. 6 (2008): 577-86.

[5]K. N. Ochsner and J. J. Gross, "The Cognitive Control of Emotion, " *Trends in Cognitive Sciences* 9, no. 5 (2005): 242-49.

Chapter 11: The Placebo Pastor

[1]See Lolette Kuby, *Faith and the Placebo Effect* (Novato, CA: Origin Press, 2003), chap. 3, www.originpress.com/placeboeffect/placebo_ch3.htm.

[2]Tim Keller, *The Freedom of Self-Forgetfulness* (Chorley, England: 10Publishing, 2012), Kindle ebook, loc. 218.

[3]Ibid., loc. 280.

[4]Judy Cannato, "The Compost Pile," *Weavings* 16, no. 1 (2001): 30.

Appendix A: The Seven-Day Personal Development Plan

[1]If you'd like to go deeper with this practice, I recommend reading James C. Wilhoit and Evan B. Howard, *Discovering Lectio Divina* (Downers Grove, IL: InterVarsity Press, 2012).

[2]Henri J. M. Nouwen, *The Return of the Prodigal Son: A Meditation on Fathers, Brothers, and Sons* (New York: Doubleday, 1992), p. 17.

[3]Dan Allender and Tremper Longman III, *The Cry of the Soul* (Dallas: Word, 1994), p. 24-25.

[4]Leighton Ford, *The Attentive Life: Discovering God's Presence in All Things* (Downers Grove, IL: InterVarsity Press, 2008), pp. 138-39, 173.

[5]Cardinal Basil Hume, quoted in Esther DeWaal, *Lost in Wonder: Rediscovering the Spiritual Art of Attentiveness* (Collegeville, MN: Liturgical Press, 2003), p. 21.

Appendix C: Research Methodology

[1] Elizabeth Skowron and Myrna L. Friedlander, "The Differentiation of Self Inventory: Development and Initial Validation," *Journal of Counseling Psychology* 45, no. 3 (1998): 235-46.

[2] Joseph Rico Drake, "Differentiation of Self Inventory-Short Form: Creation and Initial Evidence of Construct Reliability" (PhD Diss., University of Missouri-Kansas City, 2011), https://mospace.umsystem.edu/xmlui/handle/10355/11137.

About the Author

Dr. Charles Stone is the lead pastor of West Park Church in London, Ontario, Canada. He is also the founder of StoneWell Ministries, where he coaches pastors and church leaders, applying neuroscience insight to spiritual leadership. He is author of *5 Ministry Killers and How to Defeat Them*, and he can be found online at:

www.charlesstone.com
http://twitter.com/charlesstone
www.facebook.com/StonewellMinistries

IVP PRAXIS

EQUIPPING LEADERS FOR MINISTRY

"...TO EQUIP HIS PEOPLE FOR WORKS OF SERVICE,
SO THAT THE BODY OF CHRIST MAY BE BUILT UP."

EPHESIANS 4:12

God has called us to ministry. But it's not enough to have a vision for ministry if you don't have the practical skills for it. Nor is it enough to do the work of ministry if what you do is headed in the wrong direction. We need both vision *and* expertise for effective ministry. We need *praxis*.

Praxis puts theory into practice. It brings cutting-edge ministry expertise from visionary practitioners. You'll find sound biblical and theological foundations for ministry in the real world, with concrete examples for effective action and pastoral ministry. Praxis books are more than the "how to" – they're also the "why to." And because *being* is every bit as important as *doing*, Praxis attends to the inner life of the leader as well as the outer work of ministry. Feed your soul, and feed your ministry.

If you are called to ministry, you know you can't do it on your own. Let Praxis provide the companions you need to equip God's people for life in the kingdom.

www.ivpress.com/praxis